DREAM OF FLIGHT

THROUGH FEAR TO FORTITUDE

Dream of Flight: Through Fear to Fortitude is published under Catharsis, a sectionalized division under Di Angelo Publications Inc.

Catharsis is an imprint of Di Angelo Publications.

Di Angelo Publications
Los Angeles, California

Library of Congress
Dream of Flight: Through Fear to Fortitude
ISBN: 978-1-955690-97-3
Paperback

Words: Sequoia Schmidt
Cover Photo: John McEvoy
Interior Design: Kimberly James
Editors: Tenyia Lee, Willy Rowberry

Downloadable viva www.dapbooks.shop and other e-book retailers.

For educational, business, and bulk orders, contact sales@diangelopublications.com.

1. Travel --- Special Interest --- Adventure
2. Sports & Recreation --- Extreme Sports
3. Biography & Autobiography --- Personal Memoirs

DREAM OF FLIGHT

THROUGH FEAR TO FORTITUDE

SEQUOIA SCHMIDT

DAP BOOKS
DI ANGELO PUBLICATIONS

Other titles by Sequoia Schmidt:

Journey of Heart: A Sojurn to K2

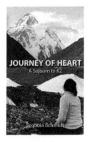

Changing Gears: Ups and Downs on the New Zealand Road

Chapters 1–8 of this book were originally published as a column called "Learning to Fly" in the *Adventure Sports Journal* in 2016. Some of the text has been reformatted to fit the publication of this book.

This book is dedicated to my mentors who guided me into the world of human flight.

To Matt Blanc and Sean Chuma, your wisdom, words, and knowledge were carried with me in every leap. Thank you for your patience, friendship, and mentorship through this journey.

Dean Potter, who continues to inspire us to live not within our minds' pre-constructed limits, but rather, push the boundaries of human flight.

And finally, to my incredible husband, John McEvoy, who has been my patient and understanding companion through the ups and downs of this process. This world has brought so many wonderful things to my life, but you are by far the best. Thank you for standing on the edge with me, holding my hand, and taking that jump — our best days are yet to come, and it is my hope that we may share many more moments together in the sky and on the ground. Thank you for opening my eyes to the true meaning of the human experience.

FOREWORD
by Matt Blanc

The most commonly given and often misunderstood advice I've heard as a BASE jumper is "take your time." Most people who hear this advice take it to mean "slow down," and perhaps that's often what's called for. But the complete meaning of "take your time" has more depth and might be easier to grasp when it's reworded to "seize your moment." For me, the intent of telling someone to take their time is to tell them to take an accounting of their desires and their needs and take action during a time where the totality of themselves (mind, body, and soul) are aligned with their surroundings. For some of us that time is now, and for others it isn't, but either way the advice is rooted in the belief that being in harmony is paramount while being in danger.

When I'm on the exit point with a slow moving group and I can see that a jumper is holding themselves back even though their moment is passing by, I look over the edge with them and say, "Take your time," and happily watch them leave us all behind. And when a group starts to pressure a new jumper to go faster than they're comfortable, I calmly put a hand on their shoulder, say, "Take your time," and hang back so they know they're not alone. In both cases, the words are the same, and the meaning doesn't change, but the effect is as unique as the person I'm talking to and the situation we're facing.

Ultimately, when it comes to BASE jumping (an activity equally likely to lead to immeasurable joy as it is to lead to unimaginable sorrow), taking our time serves to reduce the chance of soul crushing regret if it all goes sideways. Whether we take things fast or slow, what's important is that we take things at our pace, and on our terms. If a moment comes along that's all ours, letting it pass would be a tragedy. Alternatively, when the moment doesn't feel quite right, it would be wise to wait and accept that our moment may be years from now, if it comes at all.

I've met few people in more need of and, paradoxically, resistant to being told to take their time than the author of this book, Sequoia Schmidt. However, I'll admit that it's nearly impossible to judge if someone is truly taking their time until we get to know them. And when I first met Sequoia, she was moving so swiftly into the danger zone that I was on the fence about whether she appreciated the value of her life or saw the forfeiture of her life as insignificant, though it was obvious she was sitting on one of those extremes. My friends had introduced us after a day of skydiving in Southern California with sly smiles and enthusiastic tones. My best guess as to why they were so eager to get us together is that they wanted to see my reaction when she told me that she was dead set on progressing from novice skydiver to wingsuit BASE jumper in a few months. For those looking for a common reference to her proposed trajectory, that would be like going from private pilot to astronaut in one season. While I had many questions for Sequoia at that moment, several things were abundantly clear without saying a word. She was without a doubt the most stubbornly determined and insanely committed jumper I had met to date, and she was certainly not slowing down unless she was forced to.

At this point I've known Sequoia for the better part of a decade and watched her attack life like tomorrow is simultaneously never guaranteed yet always expected. Her swift execution of terrifying goals while shouldering losses that would floor most of us often leaves me wondering what I'm waiting for and asking myself, "Are the rest of us taking our time or taking too much time?" I suppose time will tell, and the real answer might only reveal itself on the last page of our stories, when we find out how and when we meet our ends.

There is freedom waiting for you,
on the breezes of the sky.
And you ask, "What if I fall?"
Oh, but my darling, "What if you fly?"
— Erin Hanson

DREAM OF FLIGHT

THROUGH FEAR TO FORTITUDE

CONTENTS

PROLOGUE

What motivates the desire to experience human flight? To jump out of an airplane? Off a cliff? Paraglide? Wingsuit? Why would someone choose to do this despite the danger — or rather, is it the danger that intrigues them?

I'm not quite sure how to answer these questions. The exploration of human flight is a very personal journey. Through the telling of my story, the goal is not to explain to you the "why" but rather what this world has taught me personally. This world of flight.

There are people who dedicate their whole life to the activities that I discuss in this book. I am not one of them. I did not actively seek this lifestyle. For those who have not read my previous books or know nothing about me, let me catch you up.

I grew up in an adventure-driven family. My father was a pararescue specialist (PJ) in the US Air Force before becoming a high altitude mountain guide, guiding some of the biggest peaks in the world. My brother was an incredible skier, climber, and also artist. In 2013 they were attempting a double ascent of two 8,000-meter mountains in Pakistan. They successfully became the first father-son team to summit Broad Peak before they attempted K2. Both my father and brother perished in an avalanche on K2 at Camp 3, on July 27, 2013.

I know firsthand the pain that this life can bring. When I say "this life," I am referring to one centered around adventure, a life that attracts a unique type of person, each on their own individual journey. People who think differently. Having grown up around that community, then subsequently leaving it for many years before reentering it on my own terms, there is one thing I have gauged: The extreme adventure communities engage individuals to question — question life, question themselves, question society. This curiosity can lead to powerful and unique connections. Often starting with simple conversations on the sojourn, whether that be hiking through the Himalayas, sleeping together in a tent at 6,000 meters, or on the exit of a big wall in Brazil. The individuals are as unique as the experiences.

This story spans over the course of eight years. In that time, I have had long periods of not jumping at all. My journey didn't start like most in this activity; my approach was a little different than most. In the beginning it was simply curiosity that brought me to human flight. When I first got my skydiving license, I was planning to only skydive and chronicle that experience in a generic adventure book. However, through a series of twists and turns, I was swept up in a journey that became my life. It wasn't until now that I felt it was time to tell this powerful story that emerged from my Dream of Flight.

PART ONE

LEARNING TO FLY

"If at first you don't succeed,
then skydiving definitely isn't for you."
— Steven Wright

THE FIRST SPARK

I can vividly remember the precise moment my interest was sparked. An interest to what? I didn't know at the time. But looking back on it now, this is where it all began.

I was eleven years old and we were home on the North Island of New Zealand. In an attempt to encourage my adventurous nature, my father took me on a tandem bungee jump just outside of Lake Taupo. I distinctly remember standing on the edge of the bridge that towered 30 meters over the water. A large lump filled my stomach, and my mind was buzzing with those pinging thoughts you get right before you are about to do something a little bit crazy.

My big brother had just taken a swan dive off the edge and I thought to myself, "If only I could be that cool."

As soon as the straps on the bungee cord were secured around my ankles, a horrifying thought entered my mind: *This bungee cord is literally made up of a whole bunch of little rubber bands.* Terrified, I looked up to my dad. "I changed my mind!" I said as we made our way to the lip of the bridge.

"Too late," he replied, as he grabbed me around my waist. I felt my stomach drop as we soared off the bridge together.

For several days following that jump, I was left with something other than just sore lungs . . . I was left with curiosity. Curiosity to explore this feeling that had rushed over me moments before the leap — or in my case, the push.

As I relived that moment on the edge, over and over again, the curiosity led me to new inner contradictions, as a debate raged in my mind. My logical thinking engaged at the highest speed possible, telling my mind and body, *This is the stupidest thing you've ever done, you are going to die if you jump again*, while simultaneously the counterpart, my spirit (or maybe my subconscious) was telling me, *You only live once and should soak up every possible human experience during this lifetime, one of which is fear. Don't let fear overcome you. What kind of person do you want to be when you grow up? One who is afraid?*

A stirring deep inside of me urged me to discover more of this feeling. It ignited a spark in my eleven-year-old mind. My decision after this encounter was that I should acknowledge my fear, know my fear, and become intimate with my fear.

And then life happened. I forgot that decision, that curiosity, that feeling, until many years later . . .

At the age of eighteen, a group of friends and I went to a dropzone for a weekend excursion. That's where I completed my first tandem skydive out of a small Cessna. This was one of the scariest experiences of my young-adult life. It wasn't simply that I would jump out of the open door of the plane, but because our plane was so small, the skydiver attached to my back informed me that while the plane was flying at altitude, we would crawl out onto the wing and just hold on for a minute before we let go and fell to our potential doom. I had only seen videos of tandems, videos where everyone is smiling as they gracefully rolled out of the door of the plane. So when my instructor informed me that we would be crawling out onto the wing of the plane, I was not exactly enthusiastic. A lump began to form in my throat, much like a small orange. I swallowed past it, nodded to my instructor while sitting on his lap, and he began attaching me to his harness. The attachment looked pretty solid. Besides, it was too late to back out now.

Holding on to the wing of the aircraft at 12,000 feet, all of the emotions from my bungee jump on the bridge came rushing back through me. I had forgotten those feelings that I had vowed to connect with years before. In the video record of this first tandem, a sly smirk drifts across my face before we let go of the wing.

Upon landing, I was overcome with the familiar rush of curiosity and vowed to rediscover my desire to acknowledge my fears, know my fears, and become intimate with them.

And then life happened. I forgot that decision, that curiosity, that feeling, until many years later . . .

Flash forward seven years. I started seeing a guy. (Isn't this how all good stories start?) Ever since he was little, he'd dreamed that one day he would fly. Since I'm from an adventure-driven family and many of my friends are mountaineers and extreme athletes pushing the boundaries in their chosen fields, I am surrounded by people who do not exactly lead "ordinary" lives. One of the personality traits similar among extreme athletes is that they don't tend to stand around talking about something, they just do it. The guy I was seeing at the time — we shall name him Seth — would continuously talk about his dream of flight. So after listening to him talk for a while, I signed us up for a course called Accelerated Free Fall, or AFF for short, which leads you through the steps to learn how to solo skydive and eventually ends with your A license. What better way to explore my fears than to attempt skydiving solo, without a chaperone strapped to my back? Little did I know the simple decision to hit "accept" on the terms and conditions of the AFF waiver would change my life path forever.

AND SO IT BEGINS

It's already hot at 9:00 a.m. in the desert of Perris, California, as we make our way across the parking lot of the large dropzone located an hour inland from the California coast. I have been living in LA for three years now and never ventured to this side of the state — they say this is the land where dreams come to be covered in dust. That pretty much sums up this area: a land of dust and forgotten dreams . . . unless you are here for the dropzone. Comprising a large runway, multiple planes, and three different parachute packing areas, the dropzone even has a bar and a pool. Military from around the world train their troops in Perris — skydivers will sit on the lawn and watch as the military boys come in for crash landings — and pros come from near and far to train at this facility. On any given weekend you will see the most famous faces in the world of human flight. In reality that means they are known by all of maybe five people, because let's face it, that world is pretty small, as I would soon come to find out.

Level 1 of the Accelerated Free Fall (AFF) program is an eight-hour instructional session followed by your first solo jump. By solo they mean not attached to anyone. You are jumping on your own, but with instructors on either side to make sure you don't pass out midair before you pull your parachute. Our introduction class is small: Seth, myself, and a slightly older man named Douglas.

We are seated in a small classroom furnished with one desk and three chairs. Diagrams of jumping procedures crowd the walls and two skydiving harnesses hang from the ceiling. I assume they are for training.

"R-O-M," our instructor writes on the board after he enters the room. "Hey guys, my name is Rom. I'm from Brazil so I speak a little funny. Welcome to your first step of learning to skydive."

In the first class Rom reviews the basics of free fall. Free fall is the term used for when you are falling through the sky before you pull your parachute. Rom proceeds to tell us about body positions, altitude awareness, equipment, and then canopy flight. Canopy flight is what it's called when you are "under canopy," which means you have pulled your parachute.

The goals of our afternoon solo jump are to establish a stable body position, maintain altitude awareness — meaning we must know how close we are to the ground, as measured by the altimeters on our wrists — and perform three practice touches of the pilot chute, which is the mini parachute you must throw in order to deploy your big main parachute. This means that our right hand will reach back and grab our parachute three times so our mind knows where it is when it's time to deploy it at 5,000 feet.

Between getting these instructions and starting our rehearsals, we walk over to the wind tunnel to get suited up in our outfits, which include a helmet, goggles, and a flight suit that makes you feel like you belong on the set of *Top Gun*.

The wind tunnel at Perris is a big cylinder, 15 feet wide and maybe 30 feet tall, through which wind is blasted at more than 100 miles per hour. This allows the participant to feel as though they are in the free fall of a skydive.

Each of us in the class is allotted two minutes in the wind tunnel. The purpose of this exercise is to get comfortable with the feeling of free fall. That way we don't totally freak out when we are by ourselves in the air. Two minutes of wind tunnel time is not going to do much to raise our comfort level, but ideally it will subdue the freak out.

Rom gives us hand signals so he can communicate with us how to adjust our bodies while in free fall. For example, the pinky and index finger straight out means to straighten your arms. Each signal assists us in making sure we maintain stability in the flying position. It's a lot harder than you think.

The most important of all signals is a single index finger out, which means PULL, as in pull your fucking parachute right now.

Another important signal is the thumb straight down. Contrary to what my instinct is telling me the thumb down means — that I'm in big trouble and about to die — it actually means to push your hips toward the earth. Pressing your hips down as much as possible will stabilize your free fall, so if you're wobbling around and swimming like a fish in the air, pressing your hips straight down will engage your core and allow your body to steady.

After the wind tunnel, we return to the classroom to revisit some of the equipment and take the final test. By this point, one thing has been drilled into our brains: the emergency procedure in the case of a malfunction of our main parachute.

- Look red
- Grab red
- Peel, Pull
- Look silver
- Grab silver
- Peel, Pull

Although this doesn't make sense written out, if you are looking straight at a parachute harness, it would. The harness has a red tab protruding on the right side of the mid chest area, and a silver handle parallel on the left. The "peel" part of the emergency procedure is to peel the handle (red or silver) away from the Velcro. Then you pull down on red to eject the parachute and pull silver to deploy your reserve. This procedure is used in any "oh shit" moment.

This is my first time ever solo skydiving. The reason we take an eight-hour preparatory course is that there is a major difference between a solo jump and a tandem jump.

Although your instructors remain by your side until you throw the pilot chute, the thing is, you have to actually throw your own chute, and once you do, those instructors are ripped away by gravity and you are left alone with 5,000 feet of space in which to navigate yourself down to safety on the ground. It is significantly intimidating.

Being that Perris is one of the largest dropzones in the world, it attracts both fun jumpers (people who simply skydive as a hobby) and international teams from all over the world (yes, competitive skydiving is actually a thing). Before hopping in the plane with a group of pros, and for our own training safety, we go over the jump procedure one more time in the demo plane set.

Rom leads us to the mock plane — which is literally the base frame of a metal plane — and one by one, we talk Rom through our jumps. It's my turn. And even though it's just a hunk of metal on the ground, as I approach the frame door, butterflies weave in and out of my intestines. Rom gives me the nod to go ahead. I step forward and begin to slowly work through the jump. With each movement I make, I vocalize my procedure: "Walk up to the door, elbows on knees, check in with the instructor, look at the wing of the plane, and step out. Count to four while responding to hand signals and adjusting body position accordingly. Check my altitude," I say looking down at my wrist. "Tell the altitude to my instructor. Do three practice touches. Check my altitude again, and tell it to my instructor every 1,000 feet. Lock onto my altimeter at 6,000 feet. Wave my instructors off at 5,500 feet. Pull my chute at 5,000 feet." I look to Rom for approval.

"Very good," Rom says. The butterflies settle.

"Time to suit up." The four of us head into the main prep area. Rom points to a metallic baby-blue jumpsuit with "Skydive Perris" written in large white lettering across the side. I put it on. There's something about a snug fitting jumpsuit that gives me Farrah Faucet feels. I strap a bulky round metal altimeter to my wrist, followed by helmet, goggles, and then step into the leg straps of the harness. I pull the main frame up to my waist before placing my arms one by one in the holsters. "Belly band first, then chest strap, followed by legs." Rom's thick Brazilian accent occupies my right ear as I follow his instructions, taking deep breaths with each deliberate movement. My hands quivering with anticipation, I pull tension on the final leg strap before straightening up and performing a practice touch to my pilot chute — just to make sure it's there.

As the plane begins to climb, that familiar lump starts to

form in my throat. Anxious, I look around and see Douglas with a massive grin on his face, just like a kid in a candy store. This lights a momentary flame to my courage.

As we reach 10,000 feet, two of the training teams open the plane door and, like paper planes in the path of a fan, they are gone.

"12,500 feet," Rom says. All kinds of curse words start entering my mind.

My job on this dive, apart from keeping myself calm and relaxed (yes, I said calm), is to be aware of the altitude, keep my body steady, follow the hand signals, and most importantly, pull my parachute.

Crouched, I start moving toward the door, followed closely by Rom. Late nights and Jamaican cocaine don't even begin to compare to the intensity of this adrenaline high.

My body is shaking. This is the feeling I want to explore — that fear I have been longing to understand.

"Ready?" Rom says.

I step toward the open doors. Unlike my first tandem, this skydive is out of a larger plane and the exit does not involve crawling to the wing, but rather just jumping out the open door. Knees shaking, I squat down and look at Rom as he gives me the okay signal. I look to see the horizon, take a deep breath . . . "Out, in . . . Go!"

The wind is deafening. My mind is scrambling.

"Head up, head up," Rom's hand signals are coming fast and strong. We are not on a tandem. This is not a scenic jump. I'm not here to enjoy the beautiful view of Earth as I plummet toward it. In fact, I shouldn't even look at the ground. My chin stays high. I steady my body as I float at a very high speed.

"10,000 feet," I yell at Rom after checking my altitude. He nods, and I begin my practice touches. My left arm reaches over my head as my right arm reaches back to compensate for the friction from the wind. My right fingertips touch the soft fabric of my pilot chute. "One!" Both arms come back to center. The motion repeats. "Two!" Both arms come back again. "Three!"

Feeling a little more comfortable, I check my altitude. "7,000 feet," I yell at Rom. Time seems to go a lot slower when you are in free fall. I would never think about or even notice three seconds going by in my daily routine, but up here, three seconds can be the difference between life and death.

6,000 feet. My eyes do not waver from the circular metal altimeter on my left wrist. At 5,500 feet, I wave my instructors off. In one fluid motion, I reach back, grab my chute, and throw. I feel a pull from above and as I slow, my instructors (still in free fall) are ripped away from me.

Try to remain calm. First thing's first. I have to check my chute to make sure there are no issues.

I look up to check that the shape, spin (hopefully lack

thereof), and float of the canopy are correct — no issues.

I check to make sure there is no damage to the main canopy.

Last but not least, I need to complete a control check.

As my adrenaline high begins to ease and make way for logical thought, I reach back and grab my toggles (controls). A hard turn right, a hard turn left, and a full flare (stop) midair, tells me that my chute is good to land.

With a deep breath, my heart palpitations dim and my shock subsides. But I am not safe yet, I tell myself. "Okay, Seqi," Rom's enthusiastic voice billows into my ear through my headset. "Time to land. Remember your landing pattern."

I begin the first of two 90-degree turns which comprise my landing pattern. There is a comfort in pulling my toggles, knowing that I'm in control of the flight pattern and responsible for my own safe landing. This is not like free fall. My mind is no longer scrambled. "Ready, Seqi? Flare! Flare!" With both hands firmly around my toggles, I begin to slowly pull down, as if pulling weights at the cable machine in the gym. As the ground is getting closer and closer, I have to fight the urge to rush my breaks but continue my slow downward pressure on the toggles. Finally, with a gliding sensation, my gluteus maximus touches the dirt.

A smile begins to appear on my face. *Holy moly, batman,* I think . . . *I'm hooked.*

THE DUST OF PERRIS

Class number two of the Accelerated Free Fall program began with an examination of the steps and procedures we learned in session one. Back to a small classroom with a table and three chairs we went. I glanced up at the two harnesses still precariously suspended from the ceiling toward the back of the room. We commenced with chanting a familiar aviation mantra:

- Look red
- Grab red
- Peel, Pull
- Look silver
- Grab silver
- Peel, Pull

Questions were being tossed in every direction to test our knowledge:

"What happens if you can see the sky through a hole in your parachute?"

Perform emergency procedure.

"You are coming close to landing; when do you flare

your toggles (breaks)?"

10 to 12 feet before landing.

"At what altitude do you pull your chute?"

5,000 feet.

"What do you do when this happens?" A picture is held up in front of me that illustrates ropes above the parachute tangled together. Just thinking about being in a situation like this makes my intestines twist like those ropes.

In the event of a line twist, I must push my forearms between the two risers and kick my legs to undo the line twist. If that doesn't work, I perform the emergency procedure and cut the chute loose.

Remember when you were a child playing on the swing set and the chains would get twisted? What would you do? I would push the chains apart and kick my legs in the opposite direction of the twist, causing my body to spin a few times until the chains above me straightened out. It's very similar to a line twist in a parachute. You must untwist the ropes above you. To do this, you simply follow the kindergarten protocol and kick your legs. I say "simply," but bear in mind you are plummeting toward Earth during this process. Keeping your cool while in free fall with a line twist is key . . . but it may cause your inner kindergartener to come out screaming.

As our plane starts to ascend toward Neverland, one of my instructors beside me reviews the program for today's jump. In order to pass this class, we are required to follow all of the same procedures from our first jump, with one addition: forward flight.

Step one, jump out of the plane. This is an important step. Then we must check our altitude and relay it to our instructor, perform three practice touches to our parachute, and then complete the main test of this jump: fly forward. Now, when you read this, you must erase the thought of Superman from your mind. Unlike Hollywood depictions of flight would have us believe, in reality to fly forward in the air, you have to move your hands backward and straighten your legs. It took multiple practice rounds for this to register in my mind and body. When the instructors said "forward," my mind kept jumping to Wonder Woman's arms thrusting into the air and that adorable outfit fluttering in the wind. A lot of skydiving is fighting your inner instincts to make your body do what you know it's supposed to do instead.

The plane door is open, the lump in my throat is swelling, and with a deep breath, we jump. I feel like a fish out of water, looking down at the world coming closer and closer. Which just makes me freak out even more. Note to self: freaking out in free fall does not help the situation! For some reason, I am reaching out in front of me to grab the air, as if that will stop my impending death. My heart is beating a million times per minute. I feel my body shaking, not out of fear but literally vibrating in the air . . . My instructor has his right arm latched firmly to my leg and his left arm is shaking my entire body to signal to me that I must push my hips down and keep my head up.

At no point during my freak out do I remember to look at my altimeter. My mind is in such a state of panic that I don't think to check my altitude, which is rather important.

After I'm finally stable enough to throw my chute, I feel the pull and look up to see the parachute beginning to open, but oh my god — it isn't quite there. There's something wrong, I can sense it. My speed is slowing to almost the point it should be. I don't see a hole in the parachute, but I can't really see beyond the twisted lines. "Kindergarten! Kindergarten!" I tell myself as my forearms come between the ropes and I kick; one full twist of my body and the chute is flying high. My hands are trembling from the adrenaline of a near death experience. I take a deep breath and assure myself that it's all going to be okay.

All I could ask myself was, *Why the hell would anyone CHOOSE to do this?* People jump out of planes to experience an adrenaline rush, yet I just had one of the most intense rushes of my life, and it was NOT fun. Concurrently as my negative thoughts toward skydiving flew through my mind, the wind started to pick up and throw me around like a rag doll. For some reason, I thought that just because I survived the free fall and the line twist, this meant I was home safe. Not even close. I still have to get to the ground, and the wind is beginning to billow my chute.

As a little girl, I would often amuse myself by taking my Raggedy Anne doll by her red pigtail braids and flinging her from side to side. Being strapped into this oversized parachute with the wind whipping me from side to side, I start to feel a deep empathy for poor Raggedy Anne.

My landing pattern begins. Confidence creeps in as I commence the slow downward motion of pulling my toggles towards the ground, flaring my breaks . . . but I'm flying too far to the left, so I try to correct it by pulling down on the right. It's too late, I'm too close to the ground . . . I land with a faceplant!

Breathing in the dust of the Perris desert valley, I wiggle my fingers and toes, and then start to move my body. Nothing's broken, no shooting pains, just a numb ego.

I am a frequent flyer — my SkyMiles membership is proof of that — but this was hands down the most traumatic experience I have ever had in the aviation sphere.

Arriving back at the main school building, awaiting my instructor to return and inform me of my failure, I wallow in embarrassment and think to myself, *Who is the one person who always helps my chin come up?* Why, Richard Branson, of course! Although we are not yet personal friends, I like to think of Richard as a lifelong mentor. Apart from his business acumen, there are so many qualities I admire in the Bransonator, and unlike some people, I won't hold the whole owning a private island thing against him.

At that moment a higher power possessed me to Google "Richard Branson Skydiving," and to my everlasting amusement, a YouTube video appeared.

Richard and his friend Per Lindstrom decided to cross the Atlantic Ocean on a hot air balloon. For this they needed to learn to skydive, in case the situation turned soggy. Some sweet soul decided to videotape Richard as he took his first two jumps . . . Suddenly, my life had meaning again. I won't give away the whole video, but essentially Richard Branson's skydives looked just as ridiculous as mine, if not more so. For your personal amusement, I strongly recommend you watch said video, titled "Skydiving Fails," on YouTube.

With Richard's help, I overcame the initial frustration with my inability to keep my cool. Then I had a realization: I made it to the ground without injury or death!

To the wind tunnel I galloped. If I was going to try and control my flight, what better way to learn than by practicing in a safe environment? The wind tunnel allows me to get the sensation of free fall and trains my brain to register what is needed to not feel like a fish out of water.

The aim of Level 2 was to keep my body steady and fly forward while staying relaxed. Needless to say, I failed my second level. Yep, failed miserably. But the wind tunnel allows me to get some much needed practice in forward flight so that during my next jump, I would know what my body needs to do. The last jump was a valuable lesson — I learned not to be concerned about how many times I fail the levels on this course, as long as I learn something new.

And most importantly, land safely.

DOLLA DOLLA BILL

"Just think of a dollar bill between your butt cheeks," Rom tells me confidently.

"Excuse me?" I say, a little embarrassed.

"When you were in free fall last time, you were not steady because your hips weren't down. Keep your hips down. The best way to do that is to squeeze your butt cheeks together just like you are trying to hold a dollar bill between them. This will level you out and allow you to stay stable." *Maybe a hundred-dollar bill would be sufficient motivation,* I think to myself.

As a woman who wears high heels and prides herself on being able to show off her feminine curves, I tend not to push my hips forward. After many years of adapting and perfecting my posture in high heels, it feels unnatural to cast that aside and throw my hips as far forward as possible. The thought of pressing my hips that far forward transports me right back to ballet class. "Suck that tummy in," my ballet teacher used to snap at us. "You are a stick. You are a single line from the top of your head to the base of your heel." The idea of curves was not condoned in ballet.

After spending some time in the tunnel last week

following my miserable second jump, I began to feel the difference between unstable plummeting and stabilization in mid-air. By applying the advice Rom gave me (i.e. the dollar bill method), I was able to correct my aerial mistakes. My body learned to adjust to stability in free fall, which gave my mind the confidence boost it needed to be willing to retake Level 2 and put myself back in the same position that almost induced a heart attack at twenty-five years old.

Due to my Level 2 failure on the first go-around, I'm taking what is called a "refresher class": a review of all the previous material from the first two classes. Following the classroom activities, I head out to meet Rom in front of the model airplane on the main grounds of the flight school. There, Rom asks me to run through my flight procedure for Level 2.

I step up to the edge of the cabin door and look down to see concrete. Once in flight, my current view of concrete will be replaced with a view of the Earth below.

Rom is on my right. "Okay, now what?" he asks in his thick Brazilian accent.

"I look at you," I reply as my movements dance in sync with my words.

"Okay, good to go," Rom says with a nod.

"I look at the wing tip . . ." My body pushes out. "Out." My body comes back inside the plane. "In." Rom and I are moving together at this point. "Arch!" I say aloud as we exit the model plane onto the concrete.

"I check my altitude. I relay my altitude. I perform three practice touches. I wait for your signal. On your signal, my arms push backward and my legs straighten. I move in a forward motion for six seconds. I pull my arms in and re-center. I check my altitude and relay it to you. If given the okay, I fly forward for four more seconds. I stabilize. I check my altitude again and lock on at 6,000 feet. I wave you off at 5,500 feet. I pull my chute at 5,000 feet."

"Okay. Great work," Rom tells me. "Remember your dollar bill, and let's go over it one more time."

We climb back into the model plane. It's an excellent training tool. You can mentally and physically prepare for what you have to do on your jump course. Perris has two of these models. One is in front of the school and the other is right next to the loading dock for the actual planes. Apart from the animated skydivers waiting to board the plane, the loading dock has a screen displaying the manifest for each round of jumpers who are heading up in that particular load, as well as the manifests for the rest of the day.

I am seated in the front of the plane today. Thick, repugnant gasoline fumes waft into my nose as the engine kicks up. I wonder how much pollution we are spewing into the atmosphere right now.

The plane takes off. We start to climb. At 1,500 feet we must unbuckle our seat belts. We do this because if anything happens to the plane below 1,500 feet, we are going down with it, *Lost* style (as in the TV series). However, if we are above 1,500 feet, we release our seatbelts so if anything happens, we can bail out and pull our chutes to make it safely to the ground while the plane plummets without us.

The instructors like to joke around a lot. For example, on my last flight, my instructor thought it was appropriate to tell me that I was missing my goggles and shouldn't be jumping. However, he told me this when I was only about two feet from the exit door. Today, the instructors are repeating the following joke: "Well, if you mess up, at least I know that I'm going to land safely." Not exactly the most emotionally encouraging words to hear at such a threshold.

We're at 12,500 feet and ready to jump. The pilot decides to circle and change his approach as the winds are blowing from the west.

"You ready?" Rom asks.

My stomach is in knots. I swallow. "Yes," I nod in response.

We step up to the door frame. I look over to Rom. He nods. I look out to the wing tip. It's there.

"Out." My body moves with my voice.

"In." My body comes back, ready to slingshot me out into the wind.

With a deep breath, I feel the wind cocoon around me. "Dollar bill, dollar bill!" I tell myself as my cheeks press together and my hips extend forward.

Then, just like that, I stabilize. My mind starts to relax a little, and it just feels like I'm floating in air.

I am experiencing my "Come to Eagle" moment. (Just to be clear, that's not actually jumping terminology, but I would like to put it into consideration for logbook lingo.) What I mean by that is, there is something very natural about the sensation of my body descending toward Earth. Well, at least more natural than my last horrific aerial experience.

There is friction in the wind, and I am able to control my flight pattern based off this wind friction. As my arms press backwards, my speed forward increases. My propulsion speed is based on my body shape. Every slight movement I make causes the wind to lift under me, sending me in my intended direction.

What an incredible feeling! I am actually flying. Really, literally flying.

PROGRESSION

I have found that tunnel time is the best way to train my body.

This morning starts out with two minutes in the wind tunnel at the indoor skydive center. My natural reaction when exiting into high winds is still to move my hips backwards rather than push them forward for my arch. Tunnel time helps support this maneuver. It's not simply my hips that I need to work on today; in order to pass Level 3 of the Accelerated Free Fall program, I must demonstrate two 90-degree turns to my instructors.

The roar of air pushing through the fans of the tunnel commences as I step into the manmade wind. My form is improving. There is more stability in my movement compared to my previous wind tunnel sessions.

When you have incredibly high winds blowing right at you, your ability to control your thought processes is swept away. I have to continually remind myself of things like "leg placement" and the "dollar bill method" in order to achieve the correct posture.

The first minute in the tunnel is purposeful. I need to allow my body to readjust to the feeling of flight.

Simultaneously I must adjust my posture so my presentation is correct. The second minute, however, my concentration shifts to practicing for my next jump, and the inevitability of turning.

Turning in free fall just takes the slightest of movements. Simply press your elbow or your hand down the right way and you will be thrust into a spin. It's learning to control that spin or balance it out that becomes the challenge.

One thing I have noticed with free fall is that the friction of the wind is much like water; you can control your direction with your movements, similar to swimming.

Remember as a child when you would stick your hand out of the car window? The music was on and the window rolled all the way down. You could feel the push of the wind as your hand left the safety of the car and entered the resistance of fast moving air currents. As your elbow and hand aligned horizontally, you could start to feel your hand stabilizing, but with just small movements you could control the direction the wind lifted or dipped your arm. The action and principle are just the same with your body in free fall.

"Present yourself to the wind," my instructor tells me. His instruction means that when we exit the plane, I will not simply push off and jump out, but rather present my body to the wind. Maintaining the right posture, I and the wind will work together.

"What are your three main altitudes?" I can barely hear his voice with the noise of the plane engines overpowering his vocal tones, but I hear the gist of what he is trying to ask.

I hold out my index finger. "2,500 feet," because it is our minimum decision altitude before beginning our emergency procedure.

My second finger comes forward. "5,000, we pull our chute."

My ring finger joins the party. "12,500, because we jump out of the plane!"

"Very good," he shouts back, then waves his hand in front of me, indicating I need to relax.

As we reach 12,500 feet, my stomach is in knots again. I take a deep, long, meditative breath and remind myself, *Just present your body to the wind. This is an incredible experience; don't rush it, don't overthink it. Be one with it.* This feeling of flight is unparalleled to anything I have experienced before. It is the feeling right before the flight that really puts me in the moment.

That moment when your foot is lined up with the door. That moment when you know that it's all up to you — your life is in your hands.

I have become so used to knowing that my surroundings are safe, to being subconsciously unaware of safety because it is always there, because it is provided for me. This is one of the blessings and curses of this day and age, and we all take it for granted. When I am in a moment where that safety is almost completely under my own control, entirely empowered . . . it's scary.

My body is presented to the wind. "Dollar bill," I tell myself as I feel the resistance of the wind forming a cloak around me. I complete a practice touch, then check my altitude. I'm at 10,000 feet. I receive a wave off from my instructor indicating I am good to start my turns.

My eyes dart to my left elbow. Pressing my left elbow down, my body starts to turn.

I counter with the right elbow to stop the turn, and then check my altitude. I receive the thumbs up from my instructor and start to turn again. Careful not to turn with my body or spine, just my arms, I glide into my 90 degrees.

Confidence and relaxation flow through me.

I hang out for a moment before looking to check my altitude. I see 6,000 feet and moving fast — a little too fast — my arms wave off my instructors and I pull.

I say "too fast" because from 6,000 feet to 5,500 feet should be locked on, then at 5,500 feet to 5,000 feet I should wave off. At 5,000 feet I pull. One swift fluid movement.

Lock on. Wave off. Pull.

Smooth is the key. If you move too fast, you will freak yourself out.

My chute opens with ease and I perform a solid control

check to make sure everything is in order for a safe, clean landing.

Flying does not come naturally to me. Believe it or not, flying does come naturally to some people — I'm just not one of them.

Failing Level 2 of the AFF program was an important lesson for me on my journey of learning to fly. As a result, I had to spend more time training in the tunnel and preparing myself mentally for each jump. Rather than carelessly throwing my body out of the plane, as I did in jump #2; I was redirected to focus and specifically visualize each skydive. Before I exited the plane, I continually repeated the reminder to "present myself to the wind," and it kept me from hurling myself out of the aircraft with all abandon.

It has been two weeks since my last jump, so I want to ensure that my mind remembers the feeling of free fall. Two minutes of tunnel time acts as a refresher.

Level 4 of the Accelerated Free Fall program is the first time that we will be truly solo. Our instructor will not be holding on to us throughout this flight. We will be flying free.

Even the idea that I shall be truly alone in the sky sends a chill through me. Fear is becoming my friend. Fear can teach me and alert me to make sure I'm properly prepared. All other elements of this jump are the same as our previous ones. We line up in the doorway. We have one main instructor to our right with whom we check in.

Once I receive the affirmative head nod from my instructor, I look toward the wingtip of the plane, then, "Out . . . In . . . Arch," and away I go.

I'm stable in the air, the intensity of the wind pressing against my cheeks for a chipmunk effect. My arm reaches around for the practice touch, as my instructor comes in front of me, wearing a smile that reassures me. I have a few nanoseconds where parts of my body and mind almost relax. A sensation of ease overcomes me, as I look up to see the beautiful horizon, the merging of sky and ocean in the distance, here I am soaring about it all. Perhaps this is what Leonardo da Vinci meant when he said his famous quote: "Once you have tasted flight, you will forever walk the earth with your eyes turned skyward. For there you have been, and there you will always long to return." For the first time in my life, I understand why people dream about this moment. But the moment quickly is over, as I don't have long to get through my drills and pitch my parachute.

"AFF is like a box of chocolates, you never know what you're gonna get," my instructor, Steve, tells me as I amble back to the skydive school facilities after touching down safely.

I passed my Level 4 with no issues.

Dan is the general manager of the Skydive Perris facility and the author of a book about human flight entitled *Above All Else*. I had the opportunity to chat with him a few jumps ago, and he imparted some sound advice. "Try and do more than one jump a day," he advised me. "It really helps to have back-to-back jumps. It helps your body and your mind."

Today I am able to follow Dan's solid advice. Today's agenda at Skydive Perris consists of a double jump.

Before we are able to get on the manifest for the next flight, we review the jump with our instructor and go over the Level 5 requirements. Rather than simply solo flying, we must demonstrate a "control of flight." We do this by completing two 180-degree turns and a forward motion flight.

This jump will also have a modified exit pattern to allow us to start becoming comfortable with alternative exits from the plane.

As the plane approaches 12,500 feet, I strap my goggles on tightly, followed by my helmet. My instructor, Steve, and I step to the edge of the plane. My right hand reaches up to grab the thin metal bar that runs along the top inside edge of the doorframe. I peer down and point out the dropzone to Steve. My body swings to the outside of the plane as my left hand simultaneously grabs the interior bar.

With both hands firmly gripping this bar, my body is now hanging outside the plane. I turn my body into the wind.

This twist feels familiar and my hips are now in alignment with the wing of the aircraft.

Looking over my right shoulder, I get an "okay" nod from Steve. Similar to the previous exits, I must indicate my exit through motion. For this exit, my indication will be through leg movements. My left outside leg swings out then back in, and both arms release as I "present myself to the wind." I'm not quite sure what happened in the moment right after I released and right before I realized that I forgot to arch, but I definitely felt a drop in my stomach that forced my auto-reaction to kick my body into perfect arch form. My heart rate begins to mellow out. My body levels out in free fall flight mode.

I perform a practice touch and check my altitude. 11,000 feet. Steve is straight out in front of me now. He signals for me to begin my turns. Like a bird uses its wing, my elbow presses against the air allowing my body to turn in flight. Once I reach approximately 180 degrees, my counter arm presses down to level my body out and stop the turning.

I check my altitude again, then begin to counter.

Steve is now approximately 10 feet from me and signals for me to begin forward motion. I do so with ease, allowing my small body movements to control my speed and direction during my flight. Human flight.

Tunnel time, mental drills and six solo jumps later, I'm finally starting to get a little more comfortable with my free fall.

After completing a full 360-degree turn, I lock on at 6,000 feet, wave off at 5,500, and then reach back and pull my chute.

Level 5 means no coms (communications). There is no radio in my ear, no instructor to guide my landing pattern and no one telling me when to initiate my flare (breaks for landing). This will be a "self-directed" solo flight and landing.

All the steps we reviewed run smoothly, but coming into the landing, my depth perception is compromised. I say compromised by inexperience because I had previously relied so much on the coms and let my instructor tell me when to flare. It's my fault for not paying enough attention on my previous five landings to be able to recognize the appropriate height at which to pull my toggles all the way down. I flare my brakes all the way down, far too early, causing an inevitable faceplant.

Another lesson learned. With a slightly gritty grin and dust misting off my pink suit, I've completed my jumps for the day. Level 5 is a success.

Although flying does not come naturally to me, I am naturally drawn to it. There is no feeling in the world like the sensation of human flight. I feel the positive energy of flying expanding into my daily life. Challenging myself mentally to focus on my flight and relax while in a free fall is starting to impact my ability to focus while grounded (literally).

Even as I sit on this plane right now, my laptop in hand, writing this book, other passengers around me ready for their coming adventure, I look out the window and watch the beautiful city of San Francisco far below me. The natural puffery of the clouds resting eye-level and the sky beckoning to me . . .

FINAL LESSONS

The last three lessons of my AFF course go rather smoothly. I am now getting a little more familiar with the process of gearing up, boarding the plane, and the long ride up. I'm beginning to wonder at what point the stomach butterflies will dissipate — 50 jumps? 150? 500? Will I ever feel at ease with the process? Or rather, if fear is the thing keeping me safe, making me alert, do I ever want to feel at ease?

It's a hot day in the Perris Valley; the sun beats down on the multitude of concrete that covers the dropzone. I manage to find some shade under a tree that looks out over a grassy landing area. Apparently it's the landing area for the professionals and experienced skydivers. The lush green grass is reserved for people who actually know how to land. Unlike my landing area, which is a vast, dusty desert, so far away from the main dropzone that they send a pickup truck to gather the baby birds after our terrible crash landings. Oh, to be one of those jumpers who simply glides into the green, green grass. Suave and cool in their demeanor, those jumpers have years of experience and hundreds if not thousands of jumps under their belts.

As I am approaching the last of the 25 jumps it takes to receive my A license, I sit and wonder if this is it for me. Will I just get the license and maybe do a few jumps after, just to say I experienced skydiving solo, and then simply go on with my life? Skydiving is a commitment; you have to be constantly jumping. If you stop for longer than a month or two, you have to do a "recurrency jump" and get retrained so they know you are safe in the sky. And the time commitment is not the only thing to consider — it's all very expensive. The equipment, the jump tickets, the coaching, the tunnel time. Is this something I really want to keep doing? I'm twenty-five years old, "living" in Los Angeles (I travel too much to even call it living), and trying to run a small business. Do I really have the time or patience to commit to becoming even semi-proficient at this activity? Not to mention, it is not exactly the safest thing I could be doing every weekend.

When I make the two-hour drive to Perris, I spend the whole day here, and sometimes even the night. There's a bunkhouse on the dropzone campus where out of town guests can stay hostel style for a small nightly rate. The last time I stayed in the bunkhouse, it was with eight other people all crammed into bunk beds, and for each and every one of them, this was their life dream. They all were envisioning being jumpers for a very long time, had committed their life to this activity. Not to mention all the people sleeping in their vans in the parking lot, traveling the world to be jumpers. Hearing these stories made me question my intentions with pursuing this. It's something that interests me, sure, but it's not like I had spent my whole childhood envisioning flying through the air. I'm not sure I'm like these people; I don't dream of flight. Perhaps I don't absolutely love it, simply because I don't feel completely comfortable in the sky just yet.

As I contemplate all this, I look out to the lush green landing area and watch the smooth landing of an experienced wingsuiter. He swoops into the grass with speed and ease, before coming to a delicate stop, almost like a fairy touching down, one dainty foot at a time. The most badass fairy you have ever seen.

I want to be that badass fairy.

And just like that, I'm hooked.

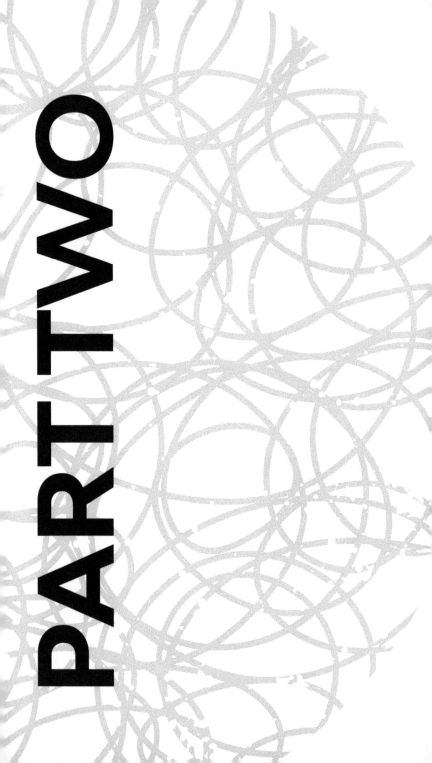

PART TWO

THE NEXT LEVEL

"If you are afraid, do it over and over again, until that fear subsides to normality." — Matt Banc

NAVIGATING THE DZ

The dropzone, or DZ, is like a classic American high school circa 1990. The facility is made up of a plethora of different social cliques. Think back on films like *10 Things I Hate About You*, *Never Been Kissed*, and even so far back as *The Breakfast Club*. Now apply that social segregation to the dropzone, but instead of being separated by personality type, it's by skydiving style.

There are various styles of jumping, and different sorts of people suited to each. There's belly fly, which is the body position you learn during the AFF course. As you grow more experienced, if you choose to become a belly flyer, you stay on your belly the whole time, utilizing your arms and legs to maneuver around the sky. Some belly flyers choose to jump in groups, which brings me to my next skydiving style: belly formation. Same flying position, meaning you maintain an arch in your back and a belly-to-earth orientation, however you are flying in formation with a team. The fun in skydiving comes in doing it in groups, and with belly formation you all wear one-piece suits with handles on them, so other jumpers can latch onto you midair. After exiting the plane, you come together as a group and create formations in the sky before breaking off to pitch your parachute. If you walk the dropzone on any given day, you will catch groups of flyers working out their formations both standing and on the ground. They sometimes lay on little skateboards to give them the belly-to-earth sensation while navigating their patterns, which they'll then attempt to recreate in the air. It's fascinating to watch. Many of the older skydivers on the dropzone will be belly flyers. It's not unusual to see people in their sixties, seventies, and even eighties spending weekends on the dropzone just doing belly fly and working on their formations. If we are to relay belly flyers into our 90s high school analogy, they would be the nerds, and belly formation would be the chess team.

Next up we have the free flyers. Think of free flying like dancing in the air. Anything from breakdancing to ballet. Free flyers swap positions constantly in flight, from sit fly (which is exactly what it sounds like, a seated position midair) to head down (where your head is facing the earth). It actually takes hours and hours of tunnel time to practice and perfect these positions, and if done proficiently, free fly can look incredible. Many free flyers will also jump in duos or small groups and follow each other's lead in positions. Similar to belly fly, they often wear one-piece suits, but with no grips for the slick sexy look, or two-piece suits with longer shorts for the cool kids. There are free flyers who amble about the dropzone totally relaxed in their long shorts, just casually swapping from sit fly to head down in the air; I would say these guys are like the skater dudes on the school campus. And then on the other end of the spectrum is the competition free flyer in their sleek one-piece suits; think of them like the dance team.

Next up we have the trackers. Tracking is where you exit the plane and simply straighten your body into an arrow for fast flight. This takes a little practice to understand how to cup your body to take advantage of the wind and gravity to increase speed. Once you understand your body's aerodynamics, you can work on things like angle tracking, which is essentially just a way to bullet towards the Earth. Often tracking occurs in groups, like a sports team. This is why I consider trackers our soccer players in the American high school analogy, and angle tracking the track and field kids.

Finally, we have the football team, the jocks, the cool kids on campus — any guess who they are on the dropzone? The wingsuiters, of course. If there's a hot guy on the DZ, chances are he flies a wingsuit. Often flying in groups, the wingsuiters generally only ever want to be with other wingsuiters. Even on the ground, it's common to see wingsuiter cliques grouped around the DZ, partially because they may be discussing their formation, and partially because there's a personality type that is attracted to each jumping style.

I went to multiple high schools throughout New Zealand, Australia and finally spent my senior year in a classic American high school in Texas. Lockers, cheerleaders, and everything! Using the same approach that got me through my classic American high school experience, my philosophy for navigating the DZ was to bounce between cliques and see what jumping style I preferred. It's not quite as simple as that though. For most of these disciplines, it takes years to become even semi proficient, and many of them have jump number prerequisites.

We board the plane, as the thick smell of gasoline and desert heat fill my nostrils. Jump number fifty-one, and I still get migraines at the end of the day from the emotional stress on my body after back-to-back flights. I can't even call them flights — I'm just falling, constantly wondering when it will start to become easier. The one thing I have noticed, however, is the difference in my exit from the plane. Now I am a little more conscious, as opposed to the earlier jumps where I couldn't even tell which way the Earth was. Crammed together on the bench, I'm with a load of jocks (wingsuit guys). Not going to lie, they are pretty hot, but much like macho football players, they are arrogant and known to be troublemakers. The one sitting next to me I know by reputation. His name is Matt Blanc and Perris is his home DZ, which means he's here all the time.

At some point in my training, I was told to notify the

wingsuiters if I am pulling at a high altitude so that they can be aware. I turn to Matt. "Hi, I'm a new jumper and I'm pulling at 6."

Matt smirks and nods his head before looking over to his buddies to relay the message.

"If you're new, you can always pull a little higher, just to be safe," Matt says over my shoulder.

Maybe I was wrong about my preconceived notions of wingsuiters. Maybe Matt understands how nerve wracking it is to be a new jumper because at some point he was in this exact position. Perhaps I should take his advice and pull nice and high.

My altimeter reads 11,500 feet as I do final checks of my equipment and lower my helmet. A smooth exit and a few seconds to get stable before I begin my drills. For the last few jumps I have been practicing summersaults both forward and backward. Since I am pulling nice and high, I only have time for two on each side before I stabilize my body, look around, and then pull my pilot chute. I take a deep breath and look up at the parachute to inspect it for issues. It looks good. All the corners are inflated, no holes, and I can reach the toggles. With a downward motion, I release the toggles and adjust comfortably in my harness to enjoy a nice smooth flight down with a beautiful view of the California coast in the distance. Just as I am starting to relax, my whole body gets thrown to one side, jerked in my harness. And before I can even begin to contemplate what happened, suddenly it happens again from the other side. Like a rocket ship is whizzing past me and knocking my big floaty parachute from side to side. When my scattered brain finally finds its peace, I look up to see two wingsuiters on the horizon. I recognize that green suit — it's Matt Blanc. I'm fuming, and the anger is just mounting as I get closer to the ground. Trying to concentrate on a safe landing, I take a deep breath to relax, because my body is literally shaking with anger. When my feet touch the ground, I don't even wait for the pickup truck to come get me, but make a beeline straight towards the grass where Matt and another jumper are laughing. The comradery continues between them, but my eyes are laser focused. As I cross onto the grass, Matt catches my eye and tries to give me a smile.

"What the hell is wrong with you?" I'm almost screaming.

The other jumper, a strapping man with reddish hair who smells of privilege and charisma, tries to chime in with a cheeky smile. "We were just having fun, you weren't in any—" But before he could finish his sentence, I cut him off.

"I have fifty-two jumps. FIFTY-TWO. I am a brand new jumper, still terrified, still learning all my systems, and you pull some fucking bullshit like that."

"It was just a flyby," the ginger says, as if I even know what a flyby is.

"Have a little curtesy, a little fucking compassion. You have no clue who I am or how I'm going to react to that." I storm off, too angry to listen to them blabbering to make excuses as I leave them in the metaphorical dust.

A few hours later, and the sun has started its slow descent. Sitting on the deck of the Perris bar with a club wrap in my hand, I'm mid-bite when a chair pulls up next to me.

"I'm Matt," he says, hand outstretched. I stare at him for a moment and continue chewing, his hand remains hovering. He flashes an embarrassed smile. "Look, I'm really sorry. You're right, that wasn't cool.".

Slowly lowering my wrap, I take a sip of water, my pace of motion glacial to let him sit in his discomfort.

His hand has now limped to the table in disappointment. "I honestly didn't think you would react like that. I genuinely apologize. Can we start over?"

There's hope in his voice, and given he's a constant figure on the DZ, I should probably let it go. "Sequoia," I say as I reach out to shake his hand.

These moments of conversation lead to hours, and before I know it, Matt Blanc is giving me advice about skydiving, starting with a canopy course. He explains to me that learning how to fly my canopy is an important step to feeling comfortable in the sky. Apparently there are a series of people who teach canopy skills, and they can help me understand some of the basics of the canopy's ability to control the parachute, figure out the stall point, and even ways to fly the canopy not using the toggles but using instead the front and rear risers (the main attachment points to the canopy itself).

Perhaps I judged Matt and the wingsuiters too quickly. Perhaps these jocks aren't so bad.

"Just be patient, keep jumping constantly, and eventually you will get better and feel more comfortable," Matt tells me.

DROPZONE DAYS

Four months later, 127 jumps in, and I'm no longer what skydivers call a "two-digit midget." But I'm still naive enough to believe I have even begun to comprehend the complexity of this sport. One would think that after more than a hundred jumps, I should know a little more about how to control my body during its flight. I mean, it really doesn't look all that hard when I am watching other people's videos, but as we all know, looks can be very deceiving. My body continues to act like a rag doll in the air, and although I understand the basic concepts of what it means to have a solid flight, my execution is still lacking in fluidity. There is no grace to my free fall, flailing arms and legs still swimming the in-betweens of the air pockets. In my mind, I have the concept of my flight, but executing that in reality is an entirely different story.

My exits for the last few jumps no longer come with an orange-sized lump in my throat or that feeling in the pit of my stomach; they're now replaced with heightened concentration. Perhaps Matt Blanc was right when he told me many jumps ago, "If you are afraid, do it over and over again until that fear subsides to normality." I'm definitely not at the point of it all feeling normal, but the fear is gradually subsiding. Perhaps I am simply looking past my fear and on to the jump itself. Although I'm attempting to do everything I can while in the air, the time of free fall is too short and it seems as though I have to pitch right before I am able to accomplish my goal for the jump. This has happened now on multiple jumps, and it ends when I land in a pile of frustration. The flight is still epic, and I still climb in the truck with a grin smeared across my dusted face, but I'm frustrated at my inability to fulfill my capabilities. In flight, as in life, unfulfilled potential is the source of my innermost frustration.

The landing of jump 128 is the moment I realized that my curiosity around fear has grown into a desire to experience flight. To truly understand where this sport can take me, I must spend some more time in a wind tunnel and get to know my body better in relation to the air. While I'm in the air, I feel what I could accomplish if only I dedicated myself a little more to understanding the intricacies of how my body, air, and gravity can help me accomplish my budding flight dreams.

FROM RUSSIA WITH AIR

It's not my first trip to Russia. Passing through the checkpoint for immigration, I get flashbacks to my visit last year, with my dear friend Hollie McKay. Hollie is a war reporter and invited me to join her on a research trip through Moscow and St. Petersburg, where she would be investigating Russian-American relations in the wake of Trump's inauguration. It was a little over a year ago now that I had to go through the task of applying for a Russian visa. At the time, Hollie was not an American citizen and was traveling on her Australian passport. Given the nature of our business in Russia, I figured it would be best if I also traveled on my non-American documentation — my New Zealand passport. However, within a few moments of conversing with the under-aggressive Russian woman at the "Russia Visa and Stamps" place a few blocks from my West Hollywood home, it became apparent that my American passport was the better option. You see, my New Zealand passport only allowed me a thirty-day stay in Russia, while my American passport gave me the option of a three-year, multi-entry visa for the cool price of $150 USD. Not knowing when I would need to return to Russia, I signed for the more open option.

This all took place long before I ever thought I would need an intense session of tunnel training, before my lofty dreams of flight were even within my grasp — back when I was a two-digit midget, potato chipping out of the back of a Caravan plane. (For you non-skydiving folks, potato chipping is when your body is so stiff and straight on your exit that the wind counteracts between your head and feet, bouncing your body back and forth like a seesaw — or like a potato chip fluttering in free fall.)

"You really need to spend some time in a wind tunnel," Dawson told me one afternoon after we attempted sit fly on our last jump. Dawson is a kid from Canada. "Kid" is an understatement; he's in his late twenties and although there is wisdom to his years, skydive banter can bring out anyone's inner child. It was a sunny afternoon at Perris. A calm breeze wrestled with the trees as we packed our parachutes for our next jump. Following his statement, I became aware that I wasn't just going to be an occasional fun jumper. I wanted this. I wanted to take it further — not just for the thrill but more so for the knowledge. He was right, a wind tunnel was necessary to get me to that next step of really understanding my body's relativity to the wind. A free fall from an aircraft would only get me a minute of good airtime, but a wind tunnel could get me hours.

"But it's so expensive," I reply.

"Go to Europe," one of the wingsuiters interjects from across the packing mat.

"Yeah, I hear Europe's way cheaper," Dawson agrees.

I was already planning to visit Europe for a few weeks this summer, and it seemed a given that when I Googled wind tunnel locations, Russia was one of the first that came up. The facility was called Freezone, and is said to have trained some of the best tunnel flyers in Europe.

If you have never seen tunnel flying, imagine it like a dance in the air. Giant fans move air upward at a speed of 120 mph — the terminal velocity of a falling human body — allowing the person in the tunnel to hover in place or use the most subtle movements to transform their body position. These tunnels were originally just a training ground for skydivers, but in recent years, tunnel flying has become more popular and has now taken on a life of its own. Some of the world's top tunnel flyers don't even bring their abilities to the sky, but choose to keep their flight within the walls of the tunnel. It's become its own sport. Sponsored flyers compete constantly all over the world but especially in Europe. They start them young now too; on any given day in Russia, you will find a five-year-old training with an instructor. The sport requires dedication and skill, finesse and elegance. Flexibility is also an asset, and the women flyers are especially captivating to watch. Being in tune with your body is essential to a successful tunnel flight, and that's exactly what I needed to work on.

In comparison to the U.S., Russia is very cheap for tunnel time. One hour in the U.S. will cost you approximately $800 to $1,000. In Russia, it's half that. And if you buy in a package, it's even cheaper. One hour may seem like a short amount of time, but in the beginning, it is not — not at all. Generally, training flights in the tunnel go for somewhere between two and five minutes. Your body cannot handle much more than that, especially at the beginning. The pressure of the air, mixed with your natural reaction to fight it, causes most newbies to get banged up pretty bad. I already know that I will be one of those newbies.

Apart from my four minutes of tunnel time during my AFF training, I've only had an additional six very expensive minutes at the Universal lot in Hollywood. I was with some friends at the movies, and as we walked out the theater, they thought it would be fun to have a go in the wind tunnel. They all assumed, with my skydiving experience, that I would knock them out of the park with my abilities. Embarrassingly that was not the case. In fact, it was me who was getting knocked out. In my three two-minute tunnel time slots, I got increasingly worse, to the point where it made me really question why on earth I spent all that time skydiving. Given I clearly did not understand my wind relativity at all, there was definitely knowledge to be gained. Solid and helpful knowledge that can be applied to the other facets of flight. Tunnel training, although prestigious in its own right, is often used as a step towards free fly — the style for jumpers who wish to focus on the form of movement in the air. Although my goals extend to more adrenaline filled forms of flight, learning just the basics of free fly will offer me an aerodynamic understanding that will surely be an asset in my future flights. Not to mention, when mastered, free fly is pure elegance. Like ballet, but in the air.

"Enjoy," the stern Russian immigration officer says with a surly smile as he hands me back my passport.

"*Spaciba,*" I say enthusiastically.

His smile lightens a touch. "*Pijousta,*" he replies. In Russia, as in most countries, if you simply make an attempt to learn the basics of the language and culture, the local's appreciation is evident.

There's a chill in the airport, but not like the first time I arrived in Russia in the heart of winter. Although beautiful, it was bone numbing. I distinctly remember the fashion — still to this day, Russia in winter had some of the best fashion I have ever seen. People dressed to the nines, no matter where they went. I saw women in Moscow wearing six-inch heels in the grocery store. Of course, like most stereotypes, this does not apply to all Russians, however I will say, Russian women have left a mark on my memories for how they carry a unique air of elegance with each step. Although the bone chill of winter is gone on this trip, the fashion seems to still remain; even on the flight, I could pick the Russian women out of the crowd, not for their look, but their

I make my way to baggage claim and load up my belongings onto a cart. "Sequoia Schmidt," the sign reads, and my eyes ride to a large, tubby, quintessentially Russian man. I wave and make my way towards him. Taking my cart, he says hello in a very thick accent and points towards the airport exit. Wheeling up to the car, I see a white Volvo imprinted with "Freezone Indoor Skydiving School" across the side. *This place is legit*, I think to myself. The ride from the airport to the facility takes approximately one hour. There I will spend the next five days of my life in intense training, learning from some of the best instructors in the world. No doubt my body and mind will be burnt out following this week, but my spirit will be flying. Literally.

The Freezone facility isn't a "facility" at all, but rather a compound straight out of the *Hunger Games*. A long, staunch building surrounded by barren Russian wasteland and a single freeway. I had heard there is not much to Russia outside of the cities, but this brings a whole new meaning to the country's vastness. It's dark by the time we arrive at the compound. White lights emphasize the lime green walls of the main buildings, rising out of the gloom like a fortress. Never before have I seen something colorful look so bleak, void of the emotion color is supposed to evoke. The words "FREE ZONE" can be seen from the turnoff point on the motorway. Two side turrets flanking the building's main entrance are painted a bold blood orange, and the building's sharp exterior lines are a tell for the personalities housed within. Culture emphasized by architecture.

Walking into the main entrance, I am greeted by the security guard and escorted upstairs. The compound reads new in its equipment, or at least very well maintained, but my guess is new. Monitors and cameras display flight trainings from the day, and up the cold metal stairs leads us to the first wind tunnel. It is big, a lot bigger than the ones in the U.S. I can feel its power without it even being turned on. A serious tone hangs in the air as I walk to the second wind tunnel. It's surrounded by training pads, workout equipment, and judging matts. This place is no joke. The Russians train hard. My generally bubbly personality takes a turn to the conservative. I have spent a lot of money and energy to be here — it's time now to get serious about my training.

On that note, I am shown to the bunkhouses and handed my key. This will be my home for the next five days. I will eat, sleep, and breathe for the wind tunnel. And with that, I close my eyes and allow my body to rest up for a beat down.

FREEZONE

The morning starts with 7:00 a.m. stretching between me and Ivan, my coach, whom I found by Instagram stalking. He and I have been in constant communication to set up this visit. Everything from the car at the airport to making sure the café had a pre-made salad for me when I arrived last night, Ivan has been my point person. This morning, Ivan is waiting for me with a warm welcoming smile when I arrive from my bunkhouse sleeping quarters to the compound facility. "Hello," he says. "My English, not so good".

"*Priviot*," I respond. "My Russian, worse."

We both laugh, and he hands me a suit. Unlike belly flight suits for group skydives, wind tunnel suits and free fly suits do not have grips on the side. The grips act as anchors for fellow jumpers to dock onto the suit. In free flight, that is not necessary. Especially not in the tunnel. This sleek red-and-white suit is form-fitting with a matching white helmet, allowing me to feel sexy for a moment, like a Daytona race car driver or an astronaut. The feeling doesn't last long. Five minutes of basic arm, leg, and body stretches, then into the tunnel we go . . . to have any feeling of sexy blown right out of me.

I almost forgot how hard this is. Tunnel flight has to be one of the most challenging but best ways to learn about your body and its natural and unnatural movements.

Growing up on this planet with gravity, everything that your mind knows about your body and its maneuvering is in relation to the gravity the Earth provides. When you alter those conditions, as you do when you're suspended in air, your natural movements suddenly require re-thinking.

The first thirty minutes is broken up into five separate sections:

1. Warm up
2. Belly fly – Balancing with upward and downward movement in the tunnel
3. Turning – Using both legs and arms, separately and together
4. Walking – Keeping a straight body position while moving your feet as if you are walking in high winds
5. Transition – Belly fly to back fly

Today I will have two hours of tunnel time. Those two hours are split into twenty sections, much like the breakdown above. Each section will have a specific concentration, and those two hours will last from 7:00

a.m. to 6:00 p.m. I know two hours spread out over a whole day may not sound overwhelming, but when you are as new to tunnel flying as I am, the muscle strength you're engaging is tremendous and it takes a lot out of your body. Not to mention you are having to recalculate your muscular tendencies in relation to the wind, which causes your body to use otherwise untapped movements. A good example of this is the angling of your knees. In everyday life, my knees naturally straighten and bend. However, in the tunnel, you have to constantly adjust your knees and hips to angle your foot horizontally away from your body. I don't know about you, but this is very unnatural to me. The angling of your knee allows for the feet and legs to act as a barrier relative to the wind, thus allowing you to turn and adjust your body with just the slightest leg movements.

The same technique is applied with your arms. When you're in the belly fly position, an elbow down, pressing into the wind, allows you to turn, while extending your hands to each side allows for a side-to-side slide. For example, if I am on the right side of the tunnel and I want to get to the left, I simply fold in my left hand while simultaneously extending my right, thus placing it as a barrier against the wind. If I then look to the left (because that's where I want to go) and apply the unnatural extension of the left knee splayed out, my body starts to move. I have to be very careful with how fast my movements happen. Move too quickly and it will cause a jerk reaction and slam me against the tunnel wall. Subtle and slow seems to be the way.

My personality doesn't really play well with slow or subtle.

The second thirty-minute session is broken into five separate sections:

1. Back fly – A concentration on balance
2. Transition – Belly to backfly via a roll and a sit transition
3. Moving sideways – While in a back fly position
4. Interactions – Work corresponding flight drills with Ivan
5. Game – Keep the level of flight steady.

Entering the tunnel is like something out of *Ender's Game*. Two thick metal doors, paned with multilayered glass, act as a security lock going into the tunnel. With the press of a button on the right side of the first door, you can hear a decompression as it unseals, followed by its opening — the sound effects alone put you in outer space. You then step into the in-between chamber, the holding area between doors one and two. Final checks to make sure everything is set: shoes tied, helmet tightened, suit zipped. And then, as if Obi-Wan Kenobi is calling you from the other side, the doors open and as young jedi in training you enter the forcefield. Okay, that's all a little dramatic, but the description deserves a little drama. It's a fricken awesome experience, or at least I imagine it will be once I actually know what I'm doing. For now however, the wind is slamming me against the wall every two seconds, and my mind is grasping for comprehension while my body is trying desperately to become familiar with unfamiliar movements.

As I exit the tunnel after my second session, the same exhaustion that takes over my body after a long climb comes over me like a blanket. I can feel each muscle and ligament starting to ache from being used in a different way than it was intended for in a gravity-native human body. Slumped on the bench next to Ivan right outside the tunnel doors, I realize this is going to be way harder than I thought. Just two thirty-minute sessions in the wind tunnel and I am already whipped. I will have exactly an hour before my next session, just enough time to rest and recoup. That is exactly what I do. Within minutes of leaving the tunnel, my aching body sprawls out on the couch, and I am knocked out.

Ivan's hand shakes my leg and I look up to see his smiling face. "Ready?" he says with an accent so thick it makes me chuckle. The Rs in English are constantly replaced with Vs from the Russian perspective.

Being the well-equipped facility that it is, Freezone has a

café area that serves those passing through. Not only folks like me frequent this facility for training of my unproficient craft, but also some of the top tunnel flyers in the world, along with local newbies who just want to experience it for one or two minutes. Tourists and Russians alike, simply wanting to have the feeling of flight. The peak hours for tourists and newbies are generally midday, and tunnel time is also more expensive during these blocks. Since I am already blowing an arm and a leg on this trip, I opted for my training to only take place during off peak hours. From 2:00 p.m. to 8:00 p.m. I shall rest, recover, and eat before my final night flight of the day. The café area is open throughout the day, and their small but adequate menu serves foods of all kinds and countries. My immediate order for my first meal back in Russia? Borsche. A soup made with meat broth and red cabbage served with sour cream and freshly chopped parsley.

My final thirty minutes of the day is focused on developing muscle memory after the six-hour break between my previous flight and now, 8:00 p.m. It is a review of all of the work we have done so far. It takes a moment upon re-entry to the tunnel for my brain to kick back into gear. Natural instincts developed over a lifetime don't just go away with an hour and a half of tunnel time, but a quick repetition of the day's work allows my mind to refocus. The first half of the evening session is to review my progress from today.

Even though Ivan and I don't speak the same language, we seem to understand each other, as communication during tunnel training happens in movements rather than words. Following the initial two minutes, Ivan is happy with my progress. I know this because he throws me a thumbs up and a goofy smile. Thus, we move on to the basics of sit fly.

Sit fly is flying in a seated position and utilizing the knees.

Between our two-minute slots of tunnel time, another group works in, a team of two French free flyers with the cool outfits to match. Their movements are fluid through the air and awe-inspiring to watch. It's hard to grasp the amount of time they must have spent to achieve that level of eloquence.

As our sessions come to an end, the French duo introduce themselves as Pier and Timothee. Their demeanor is as French as their names. It's Pier's birthday today, and based on the fact the entire Russian staff has gathered to sing him "Happy Birthday," I'd say he's a frequent flyer at the Freezone compound.

Apparently in Russia, vodka goes with everything, including and especially birthday cake, and with that the night's festivities kick off. One vodka turns into four and sails down the throat as smooth as glass. The French free flyers are staying in the bunkhouses also, and as we walk back through the stark concrete structure, they tell me they will take four days of rest before continuing their training. In just a few hours, I have grown fond of these Frenchmen. I will see them on Thursday before I depart, and we will get a day together in the tunnel again so I can attempt to mimic their fluidity in the air. Hopefully by then, my progress will be evident.

Seated on the concrete step, Timothee rolls a cigarette and proceeds to tell me about a new hotel being built in the Freezone complex, along with a wave pool. Apparently the influx in tourism to this area has justified a large investment to build out the facility.

Currently the rustic quarters of the four small bunkhouses are simple, made of plywood, with just enough room to fit a thin mattress on a wooden frame and a small bathroom. No luxury, just the necessities for rest from a hard day of tunnel training. Hard day had, I apply Tiger Balm strips across my wind-beaten body before laying down. Staring up at the patched wood-plank ceiling, a smile creeps across my face. It feels good to pour all my energy into something and come out defeated. Let's face it, the tunnel defeated me today, but putting my all into the training means that at some point, maybe in the distant future, but at some point eventually, I will get better. I roll over and turn off the naked lamp on the floor. Simple is all I need.

NO PAIN, NO GAIN

I cannot move my body. Every muscle is screaming in pain — thank god I used those Tiger Balm strips. When your body is taking a beating like mine is now, it's necessary to warm up a little more than just stretching, so I go for a jog around the parking lot.

"Morning," I greet the staunch security guard on my way up the stairs to a smiling Ivan, his eagerness approaching goofy. He has to be fast becoming one of my favorite Russians. (To be fair, I don't know many Russians.) This morning's first session in the tunnel consists of back fly transitions. The assignment is to fly on your back and then transition your body to another position. This requires both maneuvering and relaxation at the same time. Certain sections of your body must be isolated to create resistance against the wind, thus positioning the body to allow for a transition. The principle applies to any controlled movement in the air. For example, when performing a backflip in the wind tunnel, I have to compartmentalize my hips and my legs and then my head, moving them in separate sections but at the same time maintaining a flowing movement. Yes, it is as complicated as it sounds.

Let me try and break it down for you.

Basic steps for performing a backflip in the tunnel:

- First your hips must come up.
- Then extend your legs to a straight position.
- Simultaneously your head looks backwards.
- The wind then acts like a propeller, forcing your legs around and over your head to bring you back to a standing position.

This all seems to happen very quickly. To do the moves correctly, I must place certain sections of my body in the wind's path, but in order to transition smoothly, I have to relax. Relaxing in a situation like this is challenging. It requires me trusting Ivan, and most of all trusting myself. On my back, I am levitating about 3 feet from the ground, holding a steady position in the air. Ivan walks around me to assist with stability, as if he's Houdini and I am his table. Feeling confident, I thrust my hips back and my arms to the side, attempting to transition to sit fly. Just as Ivan reaches my right side, my leg swiftly shoots out in a perpendicular motion, colliding perfectly with Ivan's testicals. If you could hear sound in the tunnel, the walls would be reverberating with Ivan's scream. Horrified, I pull my hands together to put them in a prayer motion and ask for forgiveness, but my actions are too swift, throwing my body off balance. I've lost control and before I know it, the wind slams me against the hard plastic wall of the tunnel, like a bug smeared across a windscreen.

Perhaps this comes naturally to some people. I thought because of my early years of ballet and general ability to be dainty I would be able to master the tunnel. I was sorely mistaken — emphasis on sorely. With every attempted transition, the relentless wind continues to throw me against the tunnel's clear casing. I have never felt more clumsy in my life than my time in this Russian wind tunnel. It feels like I'm the punching bag in a boxing facility. Not to mention, by midday I have kicked Ivan in the nuts on three separate occasions.

It's well into the afternoon before I'm finally able to complete at least one transition on my own without colliding with Ivan (or his balls). We have slowly worked through his lesson plan for the day, and although I am beginning to trust him a little more in the tunnel, I am still navigating my way through the discomfort of the movements that tunnel flying requires.

I say goodnight to Ivan after a day of apologizing, head downstairs to the locker rooms, and jump in a hot shower. For ten whole minutes I let the boiling hot water massage my skin, and as I exit the shower I stop to stare in a steam covered mirror. Deep blue bruises line my elbows, knees, arms, and ribs like leprosy covering my body. Pain for beauty is what most say; in this case, it's pain for elegance, eloquence in the sky, for the more I seem to fly, the more delicate and agile I slowly become. I am definitely not there yet, but every bruise tallies the learning of one dainty maneuver.

"*Spasiba,*" the security guard says to me as I exit the compound and head out to my sleeping quarters. Although much of Russian culture is perceived as strong and surly, I've found the people here are very friendly. As long as I make an effort and put on a smile, they seem to do the same.

Day three. By yesterday afternoon I felt like I was starting to understand at least the basics of the tunnel, but as I go into the tunnel for the first time this morning I feel like I am relearning everything I had to learn over the last two days. It seems like the longer I spend in the actual tunnel the more I become familiar with it, but then when I exit, take a break and re-enter, suddenly my muscle memory has been erased.

Waiting for our tunnel time between sessions, I try making some friendly conversation with Ivan, for although I feel like I know him, I don't actually know anything about him.

"Are you married?" I ask. I figure if our friendship has reached the point where I am kicking him in the balls on an hourly basis, I should at at least ask the question to know if I'm permanently damaging his chances to procreate.

He looks perplexed at the question.

"Married, like a wife," I say.

He cocks his head to the side, still not quite grasping my inquiry.

If you have never tried to mime the word "married" to a non-English speaking Russian before, I don't suggest it. Finally, I point to his left ring finger, which doesn't have a ring.

A large grin breaks across his face and he nods eagerly, holding up his right hand, containing a black rubber band on that ring finger. Apparently in Russia they wear their rings on the other hand. He pulls out his phone to show me a picture of his beautiful wife and two young sons.

Good, I think, *he's already done some procreating.*

There are some very cute little puppies right outside my sleeping quarters. A mother and two little ones who seem to come and greet me each morning. This is the second morning in a row they've come running around my legs and licking my fingers, just happy to have some kind of human interaction. The puppies' father usually sleeps inside, but he's out in the mornings too, and as soon as he notices the puppies playing with me he perks up. And as the mother starts to come over, he begins to growl and bark. The more friendly the mother becomes with me, the more upset the father becomes. Extremely territorial.

Although a part of me doesn't really like the dog barking

at me, there's something beautiful about a father protecting his pack. A masculinity that's powerful and alluring. Perhaps it's my childhood trauma coming to a front, but I feel a sense of longing for many aspects of this family dynamic — the puppies playing, the mother nurturing, and the father protecting his young and his mate. The longing morphs momentarily to desire, perhaps to create this for my own life. But you know, in a human form.

These are the thoughts that occupy my mind as I jog around the parking lot in the wee hours of the warm morning in the countryside of mother Russia. My body was in pure agony waking up this morning; I could barely move a muscle without intense pain. The good kind of pain, the kind of pain that reminds you that you put in a hard day's work. Last night I applied Chinese herbal medicine patches to my body knowing full well that the day of wind beating would catch up to me. My mother got the patches for me when I first started alpine climbing, because she knew that I would need them after long hard days in the mountains. Placing the wax paper patches between my hands, I rub them back and forth to get them really warm and then apply the medicine directly to my skin. This is a nightly ritual when loading my body with hard work. The patch is infused with Tiger Balm, so it can be a little uncomfortable and tingly at first but it's very good for any aches, pains, and muscle cramps. The morning jog helps loosen up my muscles a little before I head in for another beating.

As the glass doors of the compound close behind me, I nod to the security guard before heading to the changing room. The slick one-piece suit slides over my bruises, and with each passing moment I feel more like a jedi in training. The sterile metal stairs wind up to the second floor, where Ivan is waiting for me in the café, smiling per usual. Coffee in hand, we review drills for the day. Unlike previous days where we did thirty-minute sessions, today consists of a series of fifteen-minute sessions. Thirty minutes straight was too hard on my body, and I think Ivan noticed that. Or perhaps he is preemptively protecting himself — the more tired I get in the tunnel, the more chance of a kick in the balls for Ivan. The previous two occasions happened at the tail end of our thirty-minute sessions. As we grab our helmets off the table, Ivan points to the bathroom and then holds up a white plastic cup. Not a drinking cup, but the cups they use in sports to protect men's junk. He gives me a thumbs up with a goofy smile plastered across his face. I chuckle and head towards the tunnel.

The first fifteen minutes is just a warm up, and it feels really good. Back fly, belly fly, going back and forward, sliding across the tunnel. The breaks between sessions are nice, but by the fourth session I am whipped. As soon as we exit the tunnel I lay down to take a nap and immediately I am out. I rarely dream when I nap; generally it takes a deep slumber to evoke vivid dreams. However, through the last few nights and even naps during the day, my dreams have been strong and the images stay with me as I wake. Perhaps it's the hard days of work, or perhaps it's Russia, but either way it leaves me contemplating the nature of my current reality.

My brother has been appearing a lot in my dreams. I cannot always see his face, but I know it is him. Denali.

"Aren't you scared?" I ask him

"Scared of what?" he replies.

We are sitting on the roof of a skyscraper, our feet dangling some forty stories off the ground. I rest both hands slightly behind my body on the warm concrete lip of the building's edge.

"Scared of dying," I say.

"No," he replied with a gentle smile.

Denali always knew how to make me feel safe. Perhaps it is a big brother trait, or perhaps I was just incredibly lucky to get him as my big brother.

Leaning over the lip of the building, I look down at the vast void between us and the busy city traffic below. It feels as though we are in a scene from *The Matrix*, with the cars rushing along the street so far down it looks like a miniature model of reality. That ever-familiar knot in my stomach begins to tighten. Suddenly something grabs my ankle, a jolt of fear comes over me, and my eyes shoot open.

Ivan is shaking my leg. It's training time.

I must have been out for about twenty minutes. I go straight from waking up to putting on my helmet and getting in the tunnel. We're splitting the tunnel time with a girl and her coach this time. The usual two minutes on, two minutes off, and when I say girl, I mean really young girl. No more than six years old, her tiny body simply flopping around in the tunnel. I shouldn't say flop — she flies. She's actually dainty and delicate, but the strong wind just throws her little figure so quickly that to the naked eye, it could be misconstrued as flopping. Whether flopping or flying, this little fairy is putting me to shame. Her movements are much more elegant than mine. Where I am getting jarred back and forth, she moves through the air with fluidity and control.

It doesn't help that we're working on something that I'm really not naturally good at in this session. Our third session for the day, we're working on a flip. So to flip forward, I straighten my legs and my hips go up. So my hips are naturally bent back a little when I'm in sit fly or even in back fly. But to flip, my hips have to go forward to align perfectly with my body while my legs go straight so my whole body becomes like a plank. I focus on holding my body dead straight, and then my head has to tilt backwards and it flips me over automatically with the wind. Or it should flip me over with my body's resistance against the wind. But it's not quite working the way I want. I get slammed against the wall three or four times and can really feel the bruises starting to add up on my shoulders, legs and back.With each hit I'm getting more and more frustrated. Unfortunately, I'm starting to take my frustration out on poor Ivan, who's totally taking it like a champ. He can tell I'm really tired and my body is hurting. It doesn't help that every interval we go out, I see this little six-year-old girl mastering everything she learns right away, which just adds to my internal frustration. I feel like at twenty-seven, my body is already old.

It's already fighting me when I try to learn things I still want to learn. I've been so used to living in this world with gravity that I can't really grasp the idea of not being in gravity, when in actuality, my movements in the tunnel are the very definition of gravity. It's how my body is positioned in relation to the Earth that allows the air or the wind and my movements to co-exist and intertwine. I keep thinking when I'm in the tunnel that I'm in space, and that everything I'm doing is floating around, when in reality it's the opposite. In reality, gravity is pulling me down. And because of my movements in relation to gravity, I'm able to counteract the force of gravity with the force of wind resistance and play with the aerodynamics of my body.

By the end of the day, I'm beyond wiped, but Ivan wants to push for a head down for the last session of the day.

Head down is just as it sounds — flying upside down — and it's very hard to master. In order to reach the head down position for flying, just like you do in a flip, your hips have to move forward so your body is in line and you're pretty much a plank, but then your knees have to be bent. Just imagine an upside down L. That's what your body has to look like in order to maintain stability. So as the speed of the wind tunnel picks up, the resistance from your bent knees allows you a little more control, as your hands grip the net that your head is resting upon. Then your arms stretch out in front of you to counteract your knees while your head stays down.

The general idea and the goal for this last session of the day is to get into this head down position. To learn this, Ivan starts by having me grab on to the net and flip over like I am doing an inversion in yoga. Except instead of my legs being straight, my knees are bent. It's that L shape, my body perfectly straight, legs bent at 90 degrees from my body, my hands out in front of me at another 90 degrees to counteract my legs. Holding on to the net, I let go of one hand to see Ivan grinning in front of me. He holds out his finger, and I grab on to it for guidance as I let go of the net with my other hand and hold it against the rushing air. My elbow has to press down to stay horizontal and feel the wind's resistance. Slowly my head starts to lift off the ground. My body is freaking out. My neck starts to pendulum back and forth, and within seconds I flip and hit the wall with a thud. Unlike on the ground where you just fall in a heap, here you're thrown around three or four times before coming to a stop because you can't control your body. A signal to my brain instantly tells me, *Curl into a ball, curl into a ball! Bring your knees to your chest.* As soon as my knees come to my chest, the wind has less surface area to work with and I am able to fall back down onto the net of the wind tunnel.

The entire last session consisted of this. Each time I slowly start to lift up my body, my mind starts to freak out, and I end up flipping over. Sometimes I flip onto my belly, which is really dangerous because the wind speed in the tunnel when you're doing head down is really high. So if you flip onto your belly and spread out too much, the wind will shoot straight up and way too high, putting you at risk of hitting the top of the tunnel. You then have to flip onto your back really quickly and tuck into a ball so you pendulum back down. This happened to me once and I got a stern scolding from Ivan. I definitely don't feel like I mastered head down. But by the end of the day, I had made it two inches off the ground, which was a huge accomplishment in my book.

Walking out of today's training, my brain feels like scrambled eggs and my body feels like it went one to many rounds with Mike Tyson. If I thought this morning hurt, I can only imagine what tomorrow is going to feel like.

By the end of the first session of the next day, I manage to stand on my head and lift off the ground for the first time. Like really lift off the ground. Not just once, but twice. Now that I've become a little more comfortable with it, I'm starting to relax. And just as I'm starting to gain back some confidence, and feeling as though I am really beginning to understand how the wind tunnel and my body can work together, Ivan sets a new challenge. Frustrated by the prospect of a transition to something entirely new, I hear him out.

Head up flying is the mission that Ivan lays out easily. His Russian accent is starting to bother me. Everything he says is starting to bother me, because I know this will be far from easy. The first couple tries of going head up are just as disastrous as it was yesterday going head down. My mind just can't comprehend it. I'm so far out of my comfort zone that my body and mind are perplexed all over again. It feels as though each time I try something new, my mind is just constantly rushing with negative thoughts: *What if I lift up and slam against the top of the tunnel and my brain splatters into mush?*

In the evenings I analyze whether a stream of negative thoughts is just logical fear. Meaning, is the fear coming from a place of logic? Webster defines fear as "an unpleasant emotion caused by the belief that someone or something is dangerous, likely to cause pain, or a threat." In reality it isn't entirely illogical to have unpleasant emotions surrounding the wind tunnel — my body technically could hit the ceiling, and there's a small chance that would result in my death. This starts me down the dark hole of Google: "A senior police officer has died six days after suffering head and spinal injuries in an indoor skydiving accident." "A Palos Park man is suing iFLY Indoor Skydiving company after an accident at their Rosemont wind tunnel left him a quadriplegic."

In attempting to discover the validity of my fear, the research also allows me to see the statistical improbability of death via windtunnel. Through the analysis I determine that the chances of my brain splattering all over the tunnel are not exactly high, and thus determine the primary cause of the negativity is illogical fear.

"At some point it will be easier," Ivan tells me through Google Translate on his phone as we eat our borsch soup and review videos of the shaky position transitions from the last few sessions. The facility, once cold and stark, is starting to feel familiar now. The worker thanks me with a head nod as I put down my empty bowl accompanied by "Spasiba." The last section of the day is spent in head down again, as I am now convinced that Ivan is determined to turn my brain into scrambled eggs.

Afterward, I exit the tunnel for a sound slumber, knowing full well all my recently gained knowledge will fall right out of my head as soon as I hit the pillow.

The days are a blur here in the Russian wasteland, the morning and evening color in the sky a small injection of emotion in the otherwise bleak landscape. Long days lead to early nights, and by day five I cannot even remember how long I have been here. The Freezone has been kind enough to graciously offer me an extra fifteen minutes of complimentary airtime in the big tunnel. Up until this point, everything I have done has been in the small tunnel, and I'm told there's a significant difference between the big and the small tunnels. I had an inclination that I would prefer the larger tunnel, and immediately I fall in love with the sensation of spreading my body out flat and wide to shoot up to the top, before tucking in my limbs and dropping back down. Imagine jumping up and down on a trampoline, but instead using your body as its own springboard to shoot you up and down as you lay horizontal to the Earth — a very unique kind of fun. However after a few rounds of big tunnel fun, I realize that when it comes to doing maneuvers, I prefer the small tunnel. In the smaller area, I have a little more of an understanding of where the walls are and how my body moves within the space.

The cool thing about Freezone is it has photos and videos playing on big screens all around you. So every time you're done with the tunnel, you can go over to the main switchboard and rewatch your recent session from multiple angles. It's almost like living in a futuristic society. You can pull up this big screen and use your hands as a mouse to control the angels and speed — the technology here is very impressive. As soon as I'm done with that headstand, I go over and look at the photos and videos and see where my body is positioned. My body should be straight and my legs 90-degrees perpendicular. As I'm watching my headstand transition to head down flying, I can see my body naturally wants to fold in and give up — to return to safety, to stay in my comfort zone. I watch as my mind and body visibly fight that fear wanting to take over. I have to dig deep and fight that urge to fold my body and come back to the safety of the ground. Even when I'm doing a headstand in yoga, fear does not try to become the dictator of my body. Perhaps it's because I know as soon as I lift my two arms off the net, and as soon as my knees spread apart a little, the wind resistance will push me up. As I begin to hover off the ground, that sensation is so unfamiliar that my mind, and thus my body, begins to freak out.

Being in the unfamiliar is being out of control, out of our comfort zone. As human beings, we don't like that. We do everything in our power to stay within our comfort zone, to stay with what we know. A friend said to me one time, "You will like what you like." It took me a while to get that, but I did. When I listen to a song I really like, I play it over and over again. When I drive a certain way to get to a certain destination, I take that way over and over again. When I like something, whatever it may be, I continually repeat that notion. Ultimately that continuation in that pattern of what I like becomes my normal, and therefore it becomes comfortable. And that is my comfort zone. As soon as we take ourselves out of our comfort zone, our body and our mind start to freak out. But in order to understand our body, in order to really understand our mind, leaving that comfort zone is exactly what we need to do. Taking ourselves out of that comfort zone allows us to apply the different things we learn, because everything that we learn in any situation can be applied to another. What I learn in the tunnel can be applied to the air, what I learn with aerodynamics of my body can be applied to the aerodynamics of the parachute, and so on and so forth. This practice is not just in the physical manifestation but also the mental — what I learn about freedom in the sky can be applied to the mindset of freedom in life; what I learn about navigating my fear through dissection of rational and logical determination can also be applied to emotional situations day to day.

Between sessions I strike up a conversation with a Swiss skydiver who's here training for freefly. We approach the topic of tunnel flyers versus skydivers. "Most of the people in here are not real jumpers, they are just tunnel pros," the Swiss says. It's funny because you have professional tunnel flyers who rarely skydive, and when they do periodically go up in the sky, they find themself unable to cope with the vast emptiness in comparison to a tunnel's tight quarters. It's two very different types of wind. Although it's all technically air, flying in the sky is a very different feeling from flying in the tunnel — far more natural.

There are tunnel flyers who have never even been in the sky, never even touched open air. They're simply tunnel flyers, and there is nothing wrong with that, it's just important to understand the distinct difference between the two. On the contrary, a lot of skydivers get in the tunnel and don't really know the exact transitions or maneuvers. They're used to a huge open sky, so they don't understand that often you're sliding backwards in the air when you are in a certain position. But you can really notice it in a tunnel because the tunnel is so small and you have to keep your position to avoid hitting the walls. Unlike the sky, where you're in open air and, unless you're looking at your ground relativity, you don't get any indication that you're moving forward or backward, left or right, and even then the ground is so far away it's hard to even gauge your location. So ultimately, even professional skydivers still spend time in the tunnel to pick up this sense.

Flying yourself is like you're flying an aircraft, except the aircraft is your body. It's quite fascinating that every intricate little move, even the tiniest of maneuvers, sends you in a completely different direction. Through the process of spending time in the air (whether tunnel or open) you get to learn your body and understand it in a whole different way, a way you've never known before living on the ground. That's the beauty of something like a tunnel — it shows you how to navigate this aircraft that is your body, and with so much more time than you get in a skydive.

"This is not what you do to learn to wingsuit," the Swiss man says, "but it will help you know your body, and knowing your body will help you with wingsuiting. Do you want to wingsuit?" he asks. I haven't really even thought about it.. I don't know if I'm interested or how far I want to take this journey of exploring human flight. My time at the tunnel in Russia has taught me to take it day by day. I don't know how much interest I have, but I do know that I now better understand my body in the air. And I do know that the next step is to understand my equipment and work on my canopy skills.

It's super late now, about 1:00 a.m., and the Swiss skydiver and his partner from Russia are working on their routines. The Russian is pretty much a pro. He's got hundreds of hours between skydiving and tunnel time, and it's obvious by his fluid transitions and maneuvers. The guy visiting from Switzerland is very handsome, but not really the greatest flyer. He's learning just like I am. However, he's got around a thousand skydives, even wingsuits and BASE jumps, but very little tunnel time. Tunnel time is incredibly expensive, so many skydivers who choose this as a life path (in America more so than Europe) spend all their life savings on a skydiving rig, live as gypsies, and dedicate their whole lives to flight. This means they don't really have the big budget to pay for tunnel time. If they're smart like this Swiss boy, they come here to Russia to learn more in the tunnel and then apply it to the sky.

By my last day at the Freezone, my head down flying is starting to feel a little more natural. I still can't hold the position in the air on my own for longer than five seconds. My new Swiss friend, Fabian, is splitting tunnel time with Ivan and me this morning. He tells me he has about twenty-five hours total in the tunnel, and I can see he is able to hold his head down pretty strong. It's still not nearly as graceful as the six-year-old dainty Russian girl who has put us all to shame. I was told the other day from a superstar in this industry that head down flying is one of the hardest things I will ever learn in my entire life, but one of the most rewarding. Now, after days of agony and body aches, I can see what they mean. Just the five simple seconds in the air alone with my head down, time slows down and reality morphs in a very unique way. Hovering upside down above the ground is an indescribable feeling. As I float above the net, knowing that each body movement can control my flight pattern and where I go, I am relaxed, I am calm, I am in control of my fear. Seeing the world from a different perspective, not just from the air, but seeing the world upside down, may change my view on a few things moving forward.

I always thought it was so strange that people dedicated their entire lives to this activity, but perhaps now I am beginning to understand. Fabian from Switzerland is a good example of that life dedication. He's a classic skydiver story: worked in the bustling city of Bern, in the IT department in a successful technology company. He made good money and wore a suit to work every day. Somehow along the path of his mundane but simple life, Fabian found skydiving. Within four months of achieving his A license, Fabin quit his job, sold all his belongings, and became a nomad. A skydiving nomad chasing boogies and dropzones around the world.

There's something about this lifestyle that entices you, that pulls you in. It's very hard to get away from it. The idea that human flight can do more than free the body, it can also free the mind. Free the mind from all the things that hold us down, from the stresses of life. Because you realize when you're up in the air and the fear is blown right out of you, none of that stress has ever mattered. That stress will do nothing but stifle you and make you afraid. And that fear will do nothing but hold you back. The more stress you have, the more fear you have. Fear can either shut you down or and it can ignite you. And for most of us skydivers, the fear ignites us. It's not that we're fearless. It's that we understand our fear. We become intimate with our fear when we become close with our fear.

I think that's why a lot of the personalities of skydivers involve living this lifestyle, one of curiosity and instability. A lifestyle lived a little bit outside of the comfort zone. Most people are comfortable with their house and their car and their money and their suits. But for the most part, skydivers can be comfortable in anything, in any environment. We live a life that's very understated in its elegance. The freedom we receive in exchange for time sacrificed, assets sacrificed. Because we're so used to living outside of our own comfort zones, it's okay, then, to be outside of the norms of society's comfort zone.

Perhaps jumpers just love the flight so much that they're willing to risk their lives for jumping, so why not be willing to give up your stability and comforts too? When getting into deep conversations about the meaning of flight and life, like I do often with jumpers and like I'm doing now with Fabian, I begin to question: What's worth dying for? Is living this kind of life worth dying for? "I would rather break than rust," an old-school skydiver once told me. And I think I agree with that. I don't want to have Alzheimer's when I'm ninety or a hundred. I'd rather not rust out but instead live every emotion humanly possible.

Following the deaths of my father and brother, some five

years before this moment in Russia, I made that promise to myself — a promise to experience every emotion humanly possible. The highs and the lows. Each is unique. The high of waking up to sunrise on a mountain in the Himalayas does not equate to the high of free flying head down in a tunnel in Russia. These are two different kinds of highs, two different kinds of perspectives, two alternate ways of looking at the world.

Having just returned from one of the biggest dropzone boogies in Russia, Fabian shows me a video of jumpers free flying in the dark with flares attached to their ankles so it looks like fireworks in the sky. Boogies are a type of skydiving get-together where skydivers come from around the world and partake in a few days of solid jumping. It's usually two to three days and often occurs with all-day jumps. Boogies are not always held at dropzones; often they can be held at random locations around the world — in the desert, on an island in the middle of nowhere. There's even a boogie held at the pyramids in Egypt. As long as somebody has a plane and there's a bunch of skydivers willing to partake and a few people willing to be the safety load operators, then a boogie will be made. It's essentially an excuse for everyone to get together, jump, and party. Heightened energy and heightened excitement.

Through our conversations I learn that Fabian is chasing boogies all over the world. But this one, he said, was one of the best boogies he'd ever been to. Perhaps it's the Russian vodka that makes their boogies so memorable.

As our conversation drifts back to skydiving, Fabin begins to tell me about the world of BASE and why he chooses to partake in this ultra dangerous activity. If you think skydiving is dangerous, then BASE is on an entirely different plane. Everything he is describing to me is about fear — specifically controlling your fear — which is very relevant considering all my thoughts over the last week of my tunnel training here at the Freezone. My fear has been controlling my rigidity, and once I recognize that and can simulate logical reasoning to win my mental debate, I am able to dissipate that fear and regain control of my mind. Above all else, this is an exercise of the mind. You have to let go of your thoughts. You have to let go of your emotions and your natural desire to not be in this situation. When I was doing head down, it was as though my mind was scrambling on the technical side to figure out what to do, where to move my legs, how to hold my body, but also scrambling on the mental side attempting to navigate the different ways to get out of this situation. Like I wanted it to go bad very quickly so I could fold into a little ball and be done with that portion rather than see it through, rather than push myself through my fear and mental blockage. We don't like to be uncomfortable, but through the discomfort we learn the most about what we are capable of.

PART THREE

DISCOVERING BASE

"BASE jumping is not an activity about pushing oneself or extreme action but rather one of presence and precision."

— Kristofer Munkle

DIVING DEEPER

Somewhere around 250-odd skydives, multiple canopy courses, and many days on the dropzone later, it's water training day. This is where I'm thrown in a pool with a skydiving canopy covering me like a blanket and I learn the skills to escape my potential drowning. Definitely one of my worst fears is being caught under something as it sinks on top of me and my lungs slowly fill with water, stifling my screams. With that beautiful mental picture in your head, the point of this exercise is to get me familiar with that awful feeling that haunts my dreams, and instead allow me to feel comfortable in an otherwise terrifying situation like landing my parachute in a river, lake, or ocean. Dipping into the pool, my mind is racing as the fabric falls around me, like a straightjacket slowly tightening around my body. But rather than push myself through my fear and mental blockage, the fabric hits me like a stun gun and I cannot seem to move or gather my thoughts. "This is the part where you do something," Matt Blanc calls out, "or you WILL drown." At that moment, I start to scramble.

Can I get out of my harness? Do I pull my lines to my parachute directly? I frantically grab my risers on my canopy and start gathering my lines. Meanwhile, the water resistance is making the parachute heavier by the second. I'm starting to panic.

"Not that!" Matt shouts. "Take a minute to relax."

"I don't have a minute!" I scream back as the canopy begins to weigh me down.

"Calm your mind and think about what I taught you. Where's your tail?"

Taken out of context, that makes for an interesting comment, but in this situation, it triggers my entire lesson plan. I swim out from under the weighty fabric and find the "tail" of the sinking canopy just in time. Sputtering, I drag the tail to the corner of the pool, before letting out a deep sigh of relief.

"Jesus!" I say, exasperated.

Matt walks around the pool and leans down next to me. "Let's try it again," he says.

Seven rounds later and my mind's definition of calm is aligning with my body. Repetition seems to be a theme when it comes to controlling my fear.

"Now imagine doing that not in a pool," Matt says, laughing as I drag my limp body out of the water. "Imagine a rushing river and the current is pulling you down. That's why it's important to do these exercises — and now that you are comfortable with the process, change up your environment."

The same lesson that Matt taught me that day by the pool also applied to my skydiving flights — I had become so familiar with the process of jumping and landing at Perris, I didn't think that an adjustment in landing area would affect me so much. But a few months later as I exited the small Cessna over the Swiss Alps, the all too familiar fear knotted in my stomach and encroached on my canopy time as I navigated the small landing area nestled in a gulley of a small Swiss valley.

I made a point over the next few months to bring my sky rig along on my many international travels, allowing me to jump at multiple dropzones around the world and navigate multiple landing areas. After a while I began to realize it wasn't the landing area I needed to trust but rather my own ability to control my parachute — my own skills to really understand how the canopy itself flies through the air — so that in any situation, any landing area, I could navigate it with ease.

Over the next few weeks, I weekend warrior down to Perris from my place in LA. The traffic can be a challenge but I am beginning to time my departures and arrivals just right now. All this time on the dropzone and Perris is starting to feel like a second home. The cute boys come and go, but I'm careful to keep my distance, as I'm well aware now of the stagnant saying, "you don't loose your girlfriend on a dropzone, you lose your turn." Much like the climbing community, these worlds are small with limited females. Which is great for the girls because it puts them in a position to choose from a whole slew of athletic, adrenaline-fueled men all ripe for the picking. Alas, my many years navigating small communities like this has taught me to keep my legs shut when it comes to the dropzone and to respond to all flirtation with playful escape options.

There's one guy in particular whose presence has graced the dropzone a few times over the last year that I couldn't help but notice. He's tall, handsome and full of swag, and best of all Perris is not his home dropzone, more a playground as he's passing through. Generally he's in a group of four other guys, and I haven't quite figured out what their roles are in his life yet, but I have gathered that he's the leader in their social clique. For the sake of this story, we shall call him Cullan.

Cullan grew up in Orange County, and from the little I have overheard of his conversations, he spent most of his time building his tech business and wingsuiting around Europe.

"How did your water training go?" was his opening line, as I sat at a table eating a veggie wrap one late afternoon following a long day of jumps. It was a hot day in the California desert, and Cullan's white T-shirt and blue eyes sent a cold chill down my spine.

"Wet," I answered before taking a sip of water from my

Nalgene bottle.

Our conversation slowly morphed from water training to skydiving. Cullan's experience with the European BASE scene was well rumored around the dropzone, as was his long-standing reputation as a crush for many of the female jumpers. Before I knew it we were joined by his posse, discussing their latest jumps and dream lines they want to fly, while I didn't understand most of the jargon as apparently BASE lingo differs greatly from the vocabulary of the sky world. To be honest, I didn't even really understand what BASE jumping actually was and the factors that differentiate it from skydiving, but mixed in a conversation with the cool kids of the DZ was not the right time to ask. I politely and quietly escaped to the bunkhouse, knowing full well we all had a full day of jumping tomorrow and not wanting to partake in the generally late nights of debauchery that dropzone life entails. It wasn't really my scene anymore — after a youth of partying, now I tend to dip out before the nights get too wild.

The plane is filled to the brim with jumpers, including many wingsuits and Cullen among them. We pile onto the two perpendicular benches, and I feel two arms wrap around my waist. It's Cullan sliding me closer to him on the bench. "We have to cram because it's a full load," he says.

One of the other wingsuiters in his group notices his hand has not left my side, and laughs before blurting out,

"All the ladies love his black card," finishing the sentence with a wink while looking me dead in the eye.

I stare straight back and laugh. "Black cards don't impress me, but stick a swoop landing and the boy may have a chance." I wink back.

"I'll take that challenge," Cullan whispers over my shoulder before removing his hand from my waist.

Given that I know he's leaving for Europe in a few days, I play it coy. We exchange numbers in the evening, and he tells me he will call before gently laying a kiss on my cheek.

To give context to my current situation, I have spent the last few years on the road, in a different city every week. My life moves as fast as the bullet trains I rode in Japan, so it's hard for me to maintain any kind of relationship. My interactions at this point generally fizzle as quickly as they spark. Following my last climber heartbreak, if we can even call it that, I vowed to be intentional about my interactions with people in the adventure community, and my attention in dating has turned mainly to businessmen and those with more mundane views of normality. That's probably one of the reasons that no form of dating seems to sustain. Well, that and the fact that it isn't really a priority at this junction in my life.

Cullan and I spent long nights on the phone periodically as we continued through the whirlwinds of our respective thrill-seeking lives, but ultimately, given the distance, our talks morphed slowly to that of friendship above all else — which in time I greatly valued. Maintaining distance from romantic interests seemed to be a common pattern in my life. It wasnt that I didn't want a partner, but more that through extensive travel and self development, I was becoming the best version of myself, and that's what I prioritized.

Through that process, I learned that I didn't yearn for "a better half" but rather strong relationships through multiple other avenues, namely friends and work. Those close in my life periodically expressed concern that my life was too buddy-centered, and at this stage — my late twenties — I should turn my concentration towards finding someone special. The truth is, I had a lot of special someones — one in every port. They just weren't my focus, and I made that known, which often meant the relationship would fizzle over missed calls.

FIRST BASE

A year later, in the fall of 2018, I was coming off a gnarly accident while climbing in the Himalayan mountain range of Nepal, and decided to head to one of my favorite places in the world: Ton Sai. I first came to Thailand in my very early twenties, almost seven years ago, to the climber's paradise known as Ton Sai. I vividly remember feeling strangely out of place. Back then, I worked in an office and rebelled against anything to do with climbing or adventure. Ton Sai was steeped in climbing culture. Vagabonds from around the world ventured to this tiny secluded peninsula by longtail fishing boats to spend their days climbing in the hot sun and their evenings drinking Tang beer at the pirate bar.

I remember taking the fishing boat from the dock at Krabi those many years ago, gliding through the waves, the smell of salt and the excitement of the unknown. Awestruck by the towering pillars of harsh rocks protruding from the sea, I knew this was going to be a very special place in my life for many years to come.

As the boat pulled ashore and we waded through the knee-high water onto the warm sand, I looked up to the towering cliffs surrounding the cove to see climbers up high on multi-pitch walls. I had read online that the climbers all rented bungalows in the back of the cove for $10 a night. Desperately seeking a connection to my father and brother, I planned to immerse myself in the climbing culture on Ton Sai and see if this was a life path I wanted to choose. Keep in mind this is years before I ever tried skydiving, before my life was entwined with the passion for adventure. Visiting Ton Sai for the first time ignited something within me, and I vowed to come back.

I kept that promise year after year, returning every November since then to those golden shores and small bungalows. My views and life have changed a lot in the years that followed that first visit. Now, I find comfort in the Ton Sai community and the locals that I am blessed to call friends. Each year, a group of us "regulars" return to this oasis to soak in the sun and enjoy the incredible memories we make that last for years to come. Almost like a utopian society, Ton Sai through the years has remained the climbers' hideout, away from the expanding, expensive Thai resorts full of tourist families that care more about the picture of the beach than actually being on it. There's a small disdain amongst the traditionalists who intermingle with the locals and see them as friends and not servers, even as the core of what Ton Sai was slowly erodes with commercial development.

I make my way down the long winding path that leads to the big concrete wall dividing the vagabonds from the civilized. Our very own Berlin Wall, covered in quotes, sayings and art to inspire the spirit that drives many of those who venture to the back part of the cove. Monkeys stalk your every move from their positions in the trees and atop the wall, just hoping a tourist will be daft enough to carry a plastic bag of groceries — easy for their taking. Alas, I learned my lesson with those vicious monkeys many years ago and now keep my belongings in a tightly secured pack on my back. The all too familiar smell of the small rustic restaurant named Mama's Chicken wafts through sticky air. As I pass by, I see a mane of golden hair cascade to just below the bare tan shoulders of a man in his late prime. He's sitting in a slightly rotting wooden chair on the deck of his bungalow. "Oh no, here comes trouble," he says with a big smile while looking over his shoulder. Dan is the Australian climbing god that has been gracing the shores of Ton Sai for longer than I've been alive. (Not actually, but you get my point.) As we share a long embrace, the comforting smell of sweat and climbing chalk makes me feel right at home.

I warmly greet Dan, Eggon, and some of the others with hugs and smiles all around before we all head over to Mama's Chicken for dinner.

This homey restaurant (if we can even call it that) is a staple in Ton Sai, known for their pad thai, fried chicken, and fresh fruit smoothies. The plastic chairs rest unevenly on the dirt floor, the smell of burning oil wafts from the noisy kitchen, while a heavyset Thai woman yells orders from across the dining area. She is known as Mama. Generally her grandchildren are seen running around chasing wildlife and collecting dirt, but in recent years they sit somber in the corner playing on iPads.

There's a group of about ten of us for the evening meal, familiar faces through the years of escaping to Ton Sai for transcendence and a break from reality. It feels good to be back.

"You up for Humanality in the morning?" I ask, knowing full well Dan wasn't. Humanality is a popular multi-pitch (read: very tall) climb towering over the beach with an epic cave at the top.

"I am," a voice says from the table across the way. A lean, athletic, nimble body, deep brown eyes and cheeky smile. We shall call him Munk. I don't recognize him, but I do recognize the blond boy sitting beside him, strangely not from Ton Sai. I take a closer look. "Cam?"

"What are you doing here?" he says as I make my way over to the table to give him a hug. Cam is a jumper from Perris and was over in Malaysia for a big BASE jumping event before popping here to Ton Sai.

"I come here every year. Wait, you don't climb . . . What are you doing here?"

"Jumping," Cam says.

I had almost forgotten that Ton Sai was also a destination for jumpers, much to the climbers' dismay. Climbers and jumpers don't always see eye to eye on many things, and a group of jumpers left a bad taste in Dan's mouth many years ago. Three guys had come to Ton Sai without climbing experience to explore the area for jumps. They found an area they would make for an ideal exit, but it required some rigorous climbing. One of their crew fell on the climb up, and during the fall was chopped to pieces due to the area's sharp rocks. The rest of the jumpers in his crew fled the scene, leaving the search and rescue team, along with Dan, to clean up the mess. To this day, Dan rolls his eyes when he sees jumpers.

I look over to see him rolling his eyes at Cam's comment before returning to his meal. It's not simply that single occurrence that has shaped Dan's opinions — there are many elements to BASE that you would think would align with climbing but don't. For example the ethics of that group of jumpers who left their buddy after his fatality speaks volumes to the individualistic mentality that many BASE jumpers are ingrained with. Not to mention the ethics surrounding how to be prepared before venturing into a situation. Not just for a potential fatality, but prepared in general.

After a few moments of catching up with Cam, I turn to

Munk. "Do you know how to climb?"

"Yep," he replied, nodding profusely with a beaming smile. His energy is contagious, similar in tone to how I'd imagine Peter Pan.

"Cool, let's meet at the base at 6:00 a.m."

DEATH CAMP

The following morning starts with a fresh mango, coconut, and banana smoothie from Mama's Chicken before meandering down to the beachfront. Due to the large wall separating the civilized from the uncivilized, the single metal door to the pathway through the lonesome luxurious resort that leads to the beach is a one-way entrance.You can guess which way the door swings. This often leads to the vagabonds having to time their entrance perfectly, or the more common approach, like mine this morning, of climbing the 12-foot wall. Perhaps next time the resort developers should think twice about putting up a wall to stop climbers.

I slurp down the last of my smoothie as I walk up to the base of Humanality. An eager wave from Munk, who's already in his harness. I drop my pack and pull out the rope.

"Want to lead the first pitch?" he asks.

"Nah, you got it," I reply. Under a rotating belay system, whoever does the first main pitch also does the third pitch of the climb. I have done this climb many, many times over the years, and for Munk, this is his first time. Humanality's third pitch requires the climber to climb onto a stalactite positioned about 300 feet off the ground — the word "gnarly" doesn't even begin to describe it. For any climber, this particular climb is one that you will never forget. Humanality is an iconic route, and its third pitch ends in a cave in the middle of the wall.

Munk crushes. Pure ease and grace on the wall, a natural climber with obviously a lot of experience. As I reach the cave's entrance, Munk greets me with a high five.

"That was spectacular!" he says, glowing.

I let out a laugh while clipping into the anchor, and then plop down next to Munk on the cold dusty cave floor. The morning sun is beating down on the rock around us, but the cave offers some much needed cool shade after a hard climb. I take a sip of water and use some to splash my chalk covered face. Looking out on the ocean, I'm reminded just how beautiful this view can be — pure tranquility as the deep blue sea fades into the golden shore. Coconut trees line the beaches, almost like a paintbrush had created it all. Just as my mind settles to relaxation, a loud whizzing whips by the cave, followed by a sudden bang.

I lean over the edge to see an inflated parachute gliding towards the beach, before a second figure falls straight past the cave. This time I watch the pitch. The pilot chute extracts, and for a split second I can see Cam's blond hair before the chute opens behind him, and within milliseconds the deafening bang of the parachute inflating. Before this moment I had only heard of BASE and seen videos of the jumps online. Never in my wildest dreams did I think it would be this loud, this intense . . . *I have to do that,* my mind races.

"Can I ask you something?" I look toward Munk. He nods. "What exactly is BASE? Like I know it's jumping off a cliff, but how does it differ from skydiving?"

"Great question," Munk replies in a tone too genuine to be condescending. "BASE is an acronym. The B is for building; A is for antenna; S is for span, like a bridge; and E is for earth, like a cliff. All four are fixed objects, unlike a balloon or a plane, and these four fixed objects make up the objects of BASE jumping. The primary difference between skydiving and BASE jumping is the equipment. In skydiving you have two chutes, a main and a reserve. In BASE, you only have the one."

"Fuck," I say, terrified to even contemplate the idea of no reserve, no safety.

"Yeah, it can be scary when you first think about it, but the equipment nowadays is pretty solid." The key word in that sentence being "pretty." I'm not sure I would fly in a plane where the pilot was "pretty" sober.

"Thanks," I say with a smile as I step backwards out of the cave and begin to rappel down the 300-foot sheer face of Humanality's iconic wall.

Later that evening, the climbers and jumpers

intermingle in the pirate bar as the drinks flow and the many stories of epic stoke are retold. Cam comes up beside me and puts his hand on my lower back. I playfully remove it. "I have a spare rig with me and would be open to death camping you," he says. I had loosley heard the term death camping before, which jumpers use when referring to people who enter BASE in the traditional sense.

"If there's a concrete wall to keep us climbers out of fancy resorts here on Ton Sai, then there would have to be a steel cage with a moat to keep BASE jumpers out," an old climbing friend told me earlier in the day. "The word 'vagabond' doesn't even begin to describe what they are," another friend Shannon says with disdain. She spends a lot of time around jumpers in Moab. Keep in mind I haven't really met any BASE jumpers apart from Cullan who seemed to not fit Shannon's description. Matt Blanc, Munk, Cam and the others in the group are my first real interaction with the BASE species, and they all seemed like salt of the earth people to me. Chasing freedom at all costs. Perhaps I hadn't explored the world enough to meet these wild creatures Shannon describes. Perhaps I feel drawn to experience what that community has to offer — to try to understand how they see things through a unique lens. Is that lens something you are born with, or is it BASE that changes your view on the world?

I didn't say no when Cam made the death camping

comment, but I didn't exactly say yes either. The conversation moved on to why each of the three guys at the table decided to get into the sport. Each story was deeply personal on an individual level but all shared the overarching theme of exploring human experience.

Throughout the night Cam was continuously suggestive in his actions. I remember him hitting on me often back at Perris, but that wasn't exactly uncommon on the DZ. However, in the hours that followed our initial death camp conversation, Cam's comments were progressively getting stronger and more forward. I'm flirtatious by nature — it's part of my naturally extroverted personality — but I have always been intentionally general with flirtation, in an attempt to not mislead any one individual. Cam was not my type — not even close. When a guy is my type, they will know it; I'm not exactly a subtle person.

Sitting at this wooden table, in an all too familiar place, I feel strangely unfamiliar with my emotions surrounding the conversation about BASE — an excitement mixed with unease, a new level of fear that I had not previously tapped. Even thinking of BASE as a non jumper can place you in a significantly vulnerable position. The idea that you have to survive off this single parachute, and trust that the person who packed it, the person facilitating the experience for you, is responsible for your life.

Cam's comments throughout the evening that he was

"happy to facilitate the experience for me" and that "it's a bonding experience he would like to partake in with me" in any other circumstance would feel creepy and unwanted, but in this vulnerable position, his offer gave me a strange sense of comfort.

I spent the next day climbing with Dan and the crew, but my mind wasn't in it. From the moment Cam had mentioned his extra rig, my mind had drifted to possibilities of being death camped. Throughout the day my stomach was in knots over the potential that I might step off the sheer cliff of the Ton Sai wall. What if that was it? What if I died on that jump? How would I feel about my death being a first BASE jump off? It did seem rather perfect timing that Cam was in Ton Sai with a spare rig. Here. In one of the most special places in my life. And I have the opportunity to experience this unique and life altering event. Was it fate? Was this part of my life's plan? These thoughts continued well into the evening gathering at the pirate bar. An old fisherman's net made up half the floor on the top level, strung up so people could lay in it while looking down at the bar. Perched on the end of the bar, I sip my pineapple juice while looking up at the wild jumping men, deep in contemplation.

"Oh just do it if you want to," Dan says. "I think you're an idiot, but if you feel that strongly then whatever."

"From my understanding, and I don't know much," I say, chin resting on my hand as my eyes haven't left the net, "your first jump is kinda like losing your virginity. You only get to do it once, so why not make it totally epic?"

"Well I know you well enough to know you won't change your mind. But just know I still think you're an idiot. BASE jumping is insanely dangerous. Many people die."

"Yep." My head lifts from its slouching placement on my hand, and I take another sip of my pineapple juice.

By now the boys are heading down the narrow winding wooden staircase of the pirate ship shaped bar.

"How was your climb?" Munk says, his smile as electric as ever. There's something about his energy that simply lifts my mind from pensive to engaged.

"Good, rock's a little polished in that area, but good. How were the jumps?"

"Amazing."

"I'm thinking about letting Cam death camp me." I trust Munk's character; we have shared a rope.

He hesitates before answering. "As long as you have thought really deeply."

Over the next two hours, Cam assures me that everything will be okay. We're to meet at 6:00 a.m. for the first jump, and with that, it's decided that I will be death camped off the Ton Sai wall on an early October morning.

Nervous just at the thought of what tomorrow morning will bring, I order another small pineapple juice in a can and begin to pick at the label, tearing the moist paper off piece by piece. I watch Munk walking a slackline just outside the bar, his precise foot placement and laser focus as he balances between each step on the thin line of webbing. I put some bhat on the bar and stand up from the stool, chugging the pineapple juice. Munk, seeing me leaving, leaps off the slackline with ease. "You going to bed?"

"Yeah, I figured I should get some sleep before tomorrow"

"That makes sense," he says, rubbing his shoulder.

"Did you hurt yourself jumping?"

"It's been bothering me for a while, but our climb the other day definitely didn't help."

"Want some Tiger Balm?" I ask, genuinely concerned for selfish reasons as Munk was a great climbing partner and I didn't want to lose out on some good climbs because of his shoulder.

"Will it help?"

"Helps me." I turn and start walking towards my bungalow. Munk follows me. With a quick glance back, I notice Cam's sullen side-eye from the corner of the bar.

By the time we walk up the stairs to my creaky wooden bungalow in the jungle, the rain's pitter patter can be heard all around us. Inside, a large white mosquito net surrounds the bed and takes up most of the room, my climbing gear hangs from hooks in the right corner, and resting next to a paper manuscript on my nightstand sits a jar of Tiger Balm.

I flick on the amber-yellow bedside lamp before grabbing the Tiger Balm and heading outside to find Munk in the hammock on the balcony. Between the few steps into the bungalow and returning to the balcony, rain began to pour — things move fast in the jungle. A loud crack of thunder echoes through the valley. Munk sits up in the hammock as I hand him the Tiger Balm. He opens the jar and begins to apply it to his shoulder. It's strong stuff and the smell makes my nostrils sting from two chairs away. "Do you plan on doing a proper BASE course?"

"I don't know," I reply.

"I definitely suggest you do, if you want to keep jumping, that is."

I nod and smile.

"Is there a reason you want to jump tomorrow, as opposed to waiting and doing a course or something?"

I pause to think about the fact that Munk, although genuine in intention, is probably going to judge my answer. Because he can never understand my true intention, so I cop out and simply say, "Because the timing is right."

"Do you think maybe you should be a little more cautious of the person who's taking you and what their intentions are?"

"Perhaps," I admit.

He's trying to rub the Tiger Balm on his back shoulder blade but can't quite reach, and it's beginning to bother me as much as his line of questioning. "Come here," I offer.

He rocks back and forth in the hammock before gently launching out of it to sit in the wooden armchair next to me. I dip my finger in the Tiger Balm and begin to gently rub it on his back. A sharp crack of lightning, followed by a large roar of thunder, Munk's eyes not leaving mine as I massage the balm into his shoulder. I can feel him analyzing me, searching for my soul. *We could have a beautiful love affair,* I think. Alas, Ton Sai spins a great dream, but it's a lesson I have learned before. Our worlds don't fit, so why put another crack in an already broken heart?

I blink to see my legs dangling above the busy city street below. I'm back in the matrix, my head shoots right, and there he is, my big brother, real as day. "I have no reason to be afraid," he says, his voice soothing to a younger sister's eager ears.

I take a moment to soak in his presence. "Why not?" My mind is keen to understand, for he was wise from birth.

"Think about it, Sequoia." He pauses, his eyes full of love. "Why would I not be afraid of death?"

I gaze upon his gentle features, deep blue eyes and bushy brown eyebrows, carefully analyzing his every feature. How can someone so beautiful be so kind? How can someone so good share my blood? I feel the sharp breath cut my centerplex — he hasn't aged. He hasn't aged a day. And just like that, the painful realization hits me like a tidal wave.

"Because you're dead," I say with tears pouring from my eyes. Through the watery blur I can see him smile gently.

By the wee hours of the morning, the sky has calmed from her raindance, leaving the serene silence and the unique smell of a crisp morning.

"Morning," Munk says from the hammock as I step out onto the balcony.

"You're still here?"

"I figured you would want some company for the jump" he says with a smile.

I nod while stretching. "Ready?"

He springs out of the hammock. Even at 5:30 a.m. his energy is powerful.

The approach to the exit is not for the faint of heart and takes a solid hour of trekking through the thick jungle along with large climbing sections in the sticky heat of the morning. The extra weight of a rig on your back adds even more complexity to an already nerve wracking situation.

We reach the exit around 7:00 a.m. to see the glowing morning light illuminating the breathtaking view. We are about 500 feet off the ground now, and the gear up area is a tiny section just below the exit. The guys watch closely as I inspect the gear — although I know the basics of an inspection from skydiving, a BASE rig is different enough that I really don't have a clue what I'm looking for. But the inspection at least makes me appear more confident in this decision to jump, or so I assume. *There's no backing out now,* I think. "What happens if I lose my toggle?" I know enough jargon to know that in BASE jumping the toggles can simply fly off, and there's no way to get them back.

"Well I would use the riser on the back of the canopy and try to compensate for landing, but—" Munk starts to answer but before he could even finish his sentence, Cam cuts him off.

"Just throw the other toggle and land on both risers."

"There's two schools of thoughts here," Munk replies in a calm voice.

"Well she has my gear and I'm facilitating the experience, so I say throw the toggle." And with that there was an awkward silence adding intensity to an already intense situation.

Munk puts his head down to check his leg straps and acts like Cam's tone and comment didn't just spark a fire in him, but I can see it. He's trying desperately to keep his cool for my sake, as he can tell I'm already anxious.

"Let's just all take a deep breath," Cam says.

I try to shake off the feeling and bring my concentration back to the edge of the cliff I'm about to step off from. I take a deep breath and look at Munk.

He shoots me a warm and reassuring smile. "You got this," he says, followed by knuckles.

Cam begins to gear check me. "When you're ready, say

three, two, one and then just step off."

Easy enough, I think in a sarcastic tone, but simply reply with a nod, as I have no energy to put towards speaking.

A parachute assist, or PCA, is when a jumper steps off the exit while behind them someone holds the pilot chute until it has popped both the pins out of the BASE rig and extracted the parachute. In layman's terms, that means a dude holds a string attached to the parachute and pulls it out of the container, and it's essentially a safer way of BASE jumping.

My toes creep to the edge of the small ledge. My eyes look past my shoes to see the sheer 500-foot drop below me. Raw and jagged rocks line the way down, oh so far down. I can feel the air fill my ears with every breath. I can't even swallow at this point; I don't even have a stomach left. My arms go numb . . . and all the thoughts in my head disappear.

Silence. Time seems to have slowed down and my body is in a state of calm, almost like a deep meditation. This is a beautiful feeling, a peaceful feeling. I have never felt this connected to my body before. Each minute movement is intentional and perceived — I am observing every action unfold in milliseconds.

I can feel the thought form in my head, sink to my stomach, rise up my throat and out my mouth.

"THREE . . . "

The reverberation from my ribs used as fuel for the

next . . .

"TWO . . . "

In pure clarity . . .

"ONE."

 I step off.

The longest second of my life follows in pure numbness.

Before I know it my parachute opens with a crack. I'm jolted back and dangle for a moment before realizing what I must do next. I immediately reach for the toggles and turn the parachute towards the long stretch of beach, a familiar sly smile creeping across my face once more.

ONLY TRUE
WISDOM...

IS IN KNOWING
THAT
YOU
KNOW
NOTHING

SO DREAM MY FRIEND
AND WELCOME
TO
TONSAI

I LET GO
e you want it
RIGHT, come
UTY is DOWN

PART FOUR

GETTING INTO BASE

"BASE . . . it's not for everyone!"
— Scotty Bob

PAUSE FOR THOUGHT

The weeks that follow are a blur of countries, cities, and experiences. But upon my arrival back to the States I finally have the courage to call Matt Blanc back, after his missed call and text of "call me" has been lingering on my phone and in my mind for far too long.

"Hey," he answers.

"What's new? I meant to call you earlier but life and travel, you know."

"Well, we're here now. I heard about your Ton Sai jump. How do you feel about it?"

"Good . . . I mean intense, but good. I was nervous for sure but felt super confident," I say, kicking myself after the statement.

"Confident?" The tone in his voice says it all.

"Well, not really confident, but it was a lot of fun."

"Let me ask you this . . . Do you think the decision to jump with someone who you barely know and who is not exactly respected in the community was a good idea?"

I pause for a moment to really think about my answer. "The timing with everything in Ton Sai seemed right."

"Okay, let me ask you that another way." His tone is

somber and educational as if he's a professor scolding me for coming in late. "Was the decision to do a death camp with someone you do not know, when you are still a newer skydiver, a smart decision?" He pauses for a second but before I can answer he cuts in again. "Not just someone you don't know, but someone without pure intentions and in Ton Sai, a very dangerous location due to a multitude of reasons." He wasn't wrong — the sharp rocks, close vicinity to water, and the fact that Ton Sai is remote and removed for adequate rescue all make it a dicey spot for a first jump. Not to mention I knew the intentions of the facilitator were not exactly pure.

"No, it was not what I would call smart." I genuinely mean the answer. I was so high following the jump that I didn't stop to think about the decision itself. Matt has a way of explaining things in his calm and soothing tone that causes me, a known rebel to authority, to listen.

"Okay, just as long as you understand that in BASE, your decisions have severe consequences."

Matt goes on to discuss the importance of slow progression, a frequent topic of our conversations since the day we met. Every aspect of my life is lived at a pace that most cannot comprehend. This is the way I was born, I have always moved with intent — why meander when there are so many things to do and experience? Initially that speed was simply embedded in me, but after Dad and Denali died, it became even stronger. When you lose someone suddenly, the grief that follows comes in waves. Some small as ripples and others of monumental magnitude. The waves come with different realizations — and one of the first major realizations I had following their deaths was that time can be stolen. Our time is so limited, and although I already steamed ahead in this life, the accident only solidified my notion of the value of acting with expediency.

By now, Matt knows me well enough to know that part of me — my inability to slow down. Perhaps this is why I am so attracted to BASE. It forces me to slow the world down, or better yet, it slows it down for me. Never in my twenty-seven years have I felt that calm in anything outside of a deep meditation. It generally takes me five days into an intense seven-day silent meditation retreat to feel the calm that came to me in that second on the cliff's edge.

This particular conversation with Matt is poignant, because for the first time in a long time, I am forced to listen — or I will likely wind up dead. BASE is no joke; it's something I have to be very careful to progress into. I take heed of his thoughts and advice and the conversation draws to a close with an agreement that if I wish to continue my path in BASE, I will need to go to the Perrine Bridge, located in a tiny little town in a state I have never been to. Thus, I set out on the road to Idaho.

I'll end this chapter by saying there's an article called

"Surviving to Look Back: Female Progression in BASE" written by a well respected female jumper named Katie Hansen. The article sheds light on the risks women face in BASE jumping, particularly due to being fast-tracked into dangerous situations by male mentors. It emphasizes the importance of awareness, integrity, and proactive learning in ensuring safety and progression in the sport. When the article first came out there were whispers among the men in the sport - but ultimately following my introduction into BASE I understood the narrative and still strongly agree with its message.

THE BRIDGE

The bridge is a green oasis amongst vast flatlands filled with potato farms. The Perrine Bridge, located in Twin Falls, Idaho, towers 486 feet over a gully and the powerful Snake River below. Smooth and silky, but just like that snake, the water can be deadly. On the banks of the river sit two golf courses, one on either side. A family picnic area and small park, a boat dock and kayak loading strip, some stunning hikes, multiple cascading waterfalls, and just up the river a large landing area for jumpers. BASE jumping in Twin Falls dates back to the 1980's, when people used to jump with round parachutes before BASE equipment even existed. It's the only bridge where you can legally jump year round in the United States. The only other legal bridge to jump is in West Virginia and it's only legal one day a year for a large event creatively called Bridge Day. Although the jumpers claim Twin Falls has the only legal bridge, that's not exactly true. You see, when jumpers first started hauling themselves off the bridge, there was a dispute over the land. Technically the gully area where jumpers touch down sits between federal land overseen by the Bureau of

Land Management and national park land, therefore it's not illegal, but it's not exactly legal either. It's a strange gray area that the jumpers operate in — much as they live the rest of their lives.

The picturesque small town of Twin Falls is steeped in parachute culture. Murals of jumpers line city hall and the local coffee shop even has a BASE jumper special. People travel from far and wide to see the "crazy jumpers" as they exit the bridge. In high season, on any given day, tour buses will pass through, stopping only at the bridge for crowds of Asian tourists to take photos with the jumpers.

The bridge also attracts jumpers from across the world, as for many, this is their training ground. Whether it be new jumpers like me or experienced ones getting "current" — meaning they haven't jumped in a while and need to shake off the rust — this is the spot to safely practice before heading to cliffs or buildings. The reason bridges are considered the safest of all the objects is that if something goes wrong (like a 180 malfunction, meaning your parachute opens pointing the wrong way) then you're not going to fly into a cliff or building; you just fly under the bridge and turn around. On any given day of the spring, summer, and fall, the green grass next to the visitors center just before the bridge's entrance is swarming in jumpers. By swarming I mean there are ten to twenty jumpers, which for an activity with maybe 2000 participants in the entire world, that's a lot of jumpers in one place. Other than a jumper specific event, or jump sites in Europe, it's hard to find this many jumpers in one place.

BASE jumpers are unique people. If you think of the human population as falling on a bell curve, on the left you have the tiny percentage that are really amazing and unique. They're worldly, smart, and often accomplished. These can be the Google engineers, aerospace specialists, and business owners, but not only are they high-powered professionals, they're often in touch with their spiritual side as well. These unique individuals might be described as some of the most interesting people in the world. They tend to chase experience, above all else.

Then on the far right of the bell curve is what many would consider society's outcasts. They were probably the problem children in class, and in the yearbook next to their name it says "most likely to do a stint or two in prison." These people can't hold down a job and maybe never had a stable home. Most days you will catch them drinking or doing drugs. All those who fall to the far right of the curve have a similar characteristic. They've definitely broken their mother's heart.

If we look at this bell curve of humanity and carve out everything in the middle, we are left with those two extremes. These tend to be the personality types attracted to BASE. There's not a lot of middle ground, simply the best and the worst that society has to offer, juxtaposed in this one extreme endeavor.

Enter Jester. Never was there anyone with a name so fitting as Jester. Don't get me wrong, he has a big heart, but to be perfectly clear, Jester sits on the far right side of the bell curve. A man in his late forties, although based off his lifestyle, it's impossible to tell how old he really is. Jester's wiry hair, stout physique, and twitchy personality make him a sight to behold. With similar physical appearance to a Yeti, Jester is often seen on the jumpers' green double fisting Forties or riding around Twin Falls on a beat up old bike with no helmet. He isn't exactly the elected spokesperson for BASE but he is a staple at the Perrine Bridge. Back in the '90s before YouTube was a thing, Jester was caught on camera climbing the rail of the Bigsby Bridge in Northern California. As the cops approached him, he says, "Not today," and jumps. The video then aired on a show called *America's Dumbest Criminals* — and as history would have it, that became Jester's claim to fame. Never quite having a home, for the last few years Jester has lived in a tent under the Perrine Bridge, bathing only in the murky Snake River and often coming out smelling far worse than when he went in. Jester was rumored to have had a bad head injury at one point in his life, and on a yearly basis he can be seen hiding from his father who shows up looking for him. When someone dares mention the fact that he is homeless,

Jester will shout, "I'm not homeless, you're bridgeless!"

I learned all of this over the first few days in Twin Falls. Jester wasn't hard to miss, and I was naturally intrigued considering he was following the group around like a puppy dog. Someone had brought Jester a camera at one point, and taking photos had become his schtick. Many of the first-time jumpers were snapped by Jester and then he'd try selling the pictures back to students. It would have been a great hustle, if only Jester actually knew how to use a camera.

Within the first few hours of the course, I can tell that the local jumpers look out for Jester. Some bring him food; others, like Sean Chuma, let him come out on the bridge with the class and take pictures. Chuma is considered one of the greatest aerialist jumpers in the world. Meaning he does like a million flips and looks awesome doing it. His background in gymnastics, coupled with his years of experience in BASE makes him part of an elite class of jumpers. And with experience not just on bridges, Chuma is multifaceted with vast knowledge of other areas of flight including wingsuit BASE.

Matt Blanc recommended I take Chuma's course when we were discussing next steps to a slow BASE progression. Sean was a quiet guy, steeped in knowledge but with a wall up that made him hard to get friendly with. A part of me thinks that perhaps this is due to his length of time in the sport and having lost so many friends, but perhaps he was always a little reserved.

THE UNKNOWN

The early December morning brings a chill of the familiar nerves that have periodically frequented my life these past few years since I started this journey into human flight. I drove my tan sprinter van (also known as Goldie) from the California coast across the vast empty deserts of Nevada, through Utah's rocky ranges, all the way to Idaho's potato farms. *Why would anyone live here?* I thought to myself through the drive into Twin Falls. That thought stayed in my mind right up until the bridge, and then it hit me — the beauty of the Snake River Canyon. Driving further into town, the historic old Main Street reminded me of a Hallmark movie, made up with beautiful garland wreaths on every street pole.

"Are you here for the bridge?" the lady at the local coffee shop asked when I ordered a BASE jumper special.

"How did you know?" I inquire.

"Just figured. You don't look like you're from these parts."

I smile and thank her for the coffee.

Sean's quiet demeanor is calming at the exit as we prepare for our first jumps. There's a total of six of us in the class, and to my surprise, one other girl. Female jumpers, although becoming more prevalent, are not exactly numerous.

In the middle of the bridge I can feel my hands sweating beneath my gloves as we go through a gear check one by one. Sean observes us all slowly making sure that we adequately check each other before he does a final review. I volunteer to go first, mainly because I want to get it over with, to have my stomach stop twisting in knots and return to a place of ease. Perhaps I shouldn't have had the coffee before jumping. I'm starting to second-guess myself.

"All Clear," Sean says, indicating that he has completed a gear check and I am set for a PCA. After removing my gloves and placing them in my pockets, I crawl slowly over the railing. The inch lip of concrete I am standing on is not reassuring. Maneuvering my hands to a stable grip on the frozen metal, I turn my body 180 degrees to face out to the Snake River Canyon far below. My toes dangle over the edge of the concrete ledge as I look down to see the swift water move with ease. *That's got to be cold,* I think. *Concentrate, Sequoia, just concentrate.* My eyes shoot back up to the snow covered horizon.

"When you're ready," Chuma's voice comes from behind me. I look over my shoulder to see him holding my pilot chute ready to administer a PCA.

What if my chute doesn't open? Is this how I want to die? I have far too much to do on this earth to die like this. What if I step off and simply fall to my death? My mind is racing.

With a deep breath in, I begin the countdown as the warp of time takes over me, slowing my surroundings and thoughts to an almost glacial pace.

"Three."

Eyes fixated on the horizon, not daring to take another breath in, in case I change my mind during the pause.

"Two."

Perhaps this is a metaphor for every decision you make in life. You can't be half in and half out. Once you step off that edge, your decision has been made and you must surrender yourself to the unknown.

"One."

Perhaps this is a metaphor for life itself.

"See ya."

Before the words even leave my lips, I have stepped off the edge, into the unknown. And I don't fall, I simply fly.

BLACK DEATH

The numbness of day one behind me, I crawl into bed with a strange sensation of unease. Everything had gone well with both of my PCAs for the day, and my landings were clean without issue. Even the climb out, which many say is the most difficult part of the jumps, I accomplished with ease. The jagged rocks covered in a light layer of ice, the foot placement is crucial when climbing the almost 500 feet to the top of the canyon. But my years of mountain experience meant that particular part of the day was not my greatest challenge.

Thank god Goldie is equipped with a heating system that is able to run when the van is turned off. The Idaho winters hold nights that will chill your bones and tonight is one of them. Day one is done, but there are still three long days of jumping ahead, and getting rest is essential.

Tomorrow brings a new challenge with handheld jumps. This means that the pilot chute will be in my hand rather than someone else holding it for me. So when I jump I will throw the pilot chute myself to extract the main parachute. This also means that from the moment I exit the ledge, my body will spend a second or two longer in free fall before the parachute extracts. In short, it's way scarier!

I stare at the wooden panels on the ceiling of my van and try to calm my mind once more. Using meditation techniques I am able to focus on my breathing. The fear I am feeling is not irrational; this is a very dangerous activity. Death is a regular occurrence in the world of BASE. Matt lost his closest friend in a BASE jumping accident a few years ago. They were in Turkey jumping cable cars when the accident occurred. We haven't spoken about it much, but I can see he bears the scars of grief.

After his friend's death, Matt made a film about the incident — a powerful, beautiful and heart wrenching short film that captured the soul of the pain this activity can bring. He's not the only one; Munk also told me of his dear friend and mentors passing. The all too familiar feeling of seasonal deaths that come with the Alpine community are also a pattern in BASE. It's usually during the summer months, when most serious jumpers are in Europe spreading their wings to the unknown.

In the film, Matt discusses the concept of "The Letter" — an idea that before you become a fully fledged jumper, you must write a letter to someone you love explaining why. It can be your own version of the question. Many jumpers elect to explain why they are choosing to partake in this activity. It doesn't necessarily have to be that though; it can be any kind of letter you want. The practice of the letter is to have the jumper really think about what it is they're doing, the risks they are choosing to take, and whom that decision will affect. Sean Chuma doesn't do letters in his course, but I have already thought of my letter on my own, as I felt that philosophy is an important step in entering the world of BASE.

My letter is to my grandfather. And it is my sincerest hope in life that he never has the chance to read it.

The wind sways my feet back and forth above the city streets as my fingertips press against the concrete ledge I'm seated on.

"What's it like?" I ask, eyes still fixated on the road below.

"Death?" Denali asks.

I slowly raise my eyes to meet with his. His soul, raw and pure, stares back at mine.

"Oh, my little sister." He smiles so deep I can feel the warmth wash over me with comfort. He takes a slow deep breath and looks out on the horizon. "Death is but another great adventure."

CHASING SHOWERS

The day that follows is filled with more PCAs, and even a few handhelds. Although I have been here for three days in total now, I have been living out of the van for almost two weeks. My friend Faith Dickey says that this lifestyle is about chasing showers. I knew it from the climbing community, dirtbags living out their dusty dreams. But each morning I pull up to the bridge, I see it more and more in the BASE community. It's rampant in skydiving in the sense that most fun jumpers quit their jobs and work dropzone to dropzone. Faith calls it chasing showers because when you're a nomadic soul who lives out of your car and all you want to do is chase the next adventure, with a hard adventure comes a good shower. Hence, chasing showers.

It's night three of the course and my mind feels like overcooked spaghetti. A total of four base jumps today, three of which I don't even remember. We started around 8:00 a.m. with handhelds.

The fun part is climbing over the railing, but this time I have a pilot chute in my right hand. I'm vertically challenged, and the fact that my leg doesn't really reach the ground on the other side of the railing means I have to lower myself onto a tiny inch of concrete. My hand flips to face the outside. My knuckles white with fear, face out away from the bridge. I grab the bar and my body starts to rotate. From the corner of my eye I can see the ground. A shearing jolt of adrenaline pumps through my body. I take a deep breath in through my nose and let it out slowly through my mouth. My body is fully turned now. Facing out towards the horizon. My left hand grips the railing behind me, almost directly in the center of my back so my legs have even weight distribution on either side. This way when I launch off the ledge, my body departs in one solid movement. Not thrusting my hips or my arms up, but staying really solid in my position. I look past my right shoulder to see my right hand is up. My elbow at a clean 90-degree angle, holding my pilot cute up in the air. This is my throwing arm. I check in with Sean, looking for the headnod saying I am clear to jump.

I'm a tadpole in this world of skydiving, and Sean Chuma is a fucking shark. My face looks out to the horizon. This is the moment where everything needs to become clear. Where your mind is telling your body to do something. The moment where you can't have any doubts or questions. You either do it or you don't. There's no such thing as try.

Three . . .

Two . . .

One . . .

Hips forward. Knees back. Eyes on the horizon and throw. I pitch my pilot cute with a swift flick of my wrist, and then . . . I just pray that my canopy is going to open. It does.

After four intense days of BASE, I feel as though I haven't quite got enough and hire Chuma for an extra fifth day to allow me to get the most out of my time in Idaho. By the time I leave Twin Falls I have completed seventeen jumps ranging from stowed, where the pilot chute is packed in your parachute and you have to pull back and pitch it like in a skydive, to unpacked, where the canopy is already out and you throw it up in the air like an umbrella as you exit the edge. Although I am definitely still a baby jumper, I'm beginning to feel a little more secure with each jump that I do. Ultimately I know I will need to return to this bridge soon if I wish to go to Europe later this year to try big wall tracking.

PART FIVE

IT'S ALREADY A GREAT STORY...

"When you step off the edge, it's not just gravity that pulls you down — it's also the weight of everything you've ever wanted to overcome. In that moment, you're as free as you'll ever be."

— Taz

AND SO, WE MEET.

Over the next six months that followed, I chased showers from climbing volcanoes in South America to paragliding in Switzerland. March brought a new activity I had never tried before: speed riding, which is a whole other experience of human flight. Deep in the French Alps lies a little town called Valfréjus, and if Twin Falls is where people go to learn BASE, then Valfréjus is where people go to learn speed riding.

Essentially it's skiing, except instead of just skis you also have a small canopy stretched above your head. You ski super fast down a mountain and when you come to a cliff you can take off and fly for a while. It's wicked fun. It quickly became one of my favorite activities and Valfréjus one of my favorite places to visit. Not just for the speed riding but also for the markets on Wednesday full of the creamiest melt-in-your-mouth cheeses and saltiest meats you have ever had, not to mention the sweet taste of large chocolate bars cut into cubes with a wire string. Oh the French Alps — what a place to behold!

Upon returning to California in the early summer of

2019, my thoughts pulled me back to the sky. I put on a wingsuit for the first time, and quickly realized that without a suit, I was simply falling, and the wingsuit helps me fly as a literal bird in the sky. My body becomes an airplane, my arms, now full wings that allow me to navigate in a whole new dimension. But simply skydiving wasn't enough anymore — even in a wingsuit. The sensation was nothing like I have ever experienced, but even on the dropzone the true jumpers simply skydive their wingsuits as practice — they're training for BASE.

Coincidentally as my few days of wingsuiting already had me longing to try another BASE jump, Sean Chuma sent me a message mentioning that he has an extra slot available in his European course, learning to jump big cliffs in the Italian dolomites.

Thus, my life became all about preparing for Europe and the chance of going big wall BASE jumping. This meant the early parts of July were spent as a weekend warrior on the dropzone, where I floated about in a two-piece tracking suit. Some call it a sausage suit, because you look like a fat sausage in it, and mine is a Sumo 2, and it's a beautiful cobalt blue and bright yellow. The two-piece suit inflates with air when you are jumping, allowing you to get more glide and taking you farther away from the cliff. I did this continuously until finally I was at a point where I was ready for the next stage: a hot air balloon jump.

Jumping from a hot air balloon means you have the simulation of a fixed object (unlike jumping out of a moving plane). This allows you to get the sensation of a BASE jump with the height and safety of a low skydive. One weekend in late July at Perris I completed my first balloon jump in order to get used to taking my tracking suit off a "fixed" object. My morning balloon jump did not quite go as planned, perhaps because it was all so new to me or perhaps because with the early morning of July 27th came the all too familiar feeling of grief, as this was the day that Dad and Denali disappeared into K2 forever.

The jump was shakey to say the least — instead of having my hands in front of me, I had them behind me and my body went completely head down. This is not not the way to do a balloon jump or any type of tracking jump, for that matter. I think the nerves of it being my first balloon jump was the reason it didn't go over so well. So I returned to the dropzone and reverted to jumping in a suit the rest of the day just to get used to things going right again.

My gear needed a repack from a certified rigger, so I took it over to the loft to get it checked out. While I'm there, Tony, the Rastafarian Greek who runs the rigging loft, invites me over for a barbecue at his place, and I gladly oblige. Anyone who has lost someone close knows there are three days of the year that make the grief especially hard: holidays (for me it's Christmas), their birthdays, and the anniversary of their death. Today, I could use this BBQ as a good old distraction.

Tony lives in a place called the Ghetto. The Ghetto is a parking lot right across from Skydive Perris where a strange mix of vagabonds have made somewhat of a home in their mobile trailers. It's called the Ghetto for a reason, but the area has surprisingly beautiful gardens with fresh vegetables and people barbecuing. Outside, I sit at a cream colored plastic table with Antonis and we chain smoke European tobacco that I brought back with me from France. Around the side of a white Dodge Sprinter comes a scruffy, shirtless man with tattoos across his arms and one leg. He sits down next to me but doesn't say much, a little shy. *Perhaps he's just antisocial?* I think. *The strong silent type.* After a few moments of side-eyeing him, our gazes meet for a split second. Not one to be timid myself, I strike up a conversation.

"You don't look like you belong here. Where are you from?" I ask.

"Ireland. But I lived in New Zealand for a while as well before moving to Boston." I'm intrigued already. Not only is he handsome, but it turns out after coming to the States, he owned a CrossFit gym in Boston before finding BASE. Then, like all others in the Ghetto, he sold all his earthly belongings and dedicated his entire existence to BASE jumping.

After John (that's his name) uprooted his life and became a full time vagabond, he began working in the sky industry as a rigger in the loft with Tony. *He's intriguing,* I think. I want to know more about him, and the conversation flows naturally between us. Before I realize it, two hours have passed and it's getting late. When the conversation comes to a natural stopping point, I stand up and say goodnight to everyone around the table. I turn to John and place a kiss on his cheek. He looks up at me and smiles. Then, like Cinderella, I disappear.

WHEN YOU KNOW, YOU KNOW . . .

Two days later a suggested friend prompt for John McEvoy appeared on my Facebook and without thinking, I clicked "Request."

A few minutes later . . .

John is waving at you!

Me
How was your jump?

John
It was fun. I'm pretty over that jump but it's all we have close so I won't complain too much.
How was yours?

Me
Lol fair enough! It was epic . . . my body position was off tho. Definitely need to do a few more before Brento.

John
Yeah more is always better but you'll be fine.
Brento is basically a skydive.
Like you go through all the fear of a BASE jump but after the exit it feels like a skydive, just better visuals haha

Me

Haha okay good to know!

John

When you headed to Euro?

Me

I'm on my way to Yosemite now. Then have a meeting back in LA . . . then to the bridge.

John

Oh sick. Climbing yeah? I went there for the first time last month and my head exploded haha

Me

Yeah it's pretty dope! A little climbing, then hang with my aunt and uncle at their place in Bear Valley.

U know what I think, I think that u should come jump the bridge next week.

John

Oh you do, do you? Hahaha

What days are you going? Driving?

Me

My vans going to stay up here — prolly in Reno — I have a meeting in LA on Wednesday and Thursday, a speech in Texas on Friday, then I have to be back in LA on Saturday, I'll probably do a balloon jump on Sunday . . . then I think I'll fly to Reno and pick up my van then head up to the bridge, I'll be up at the bridge for like a week. That's my rough schedule

John

Damn you a busy lady!

Depending on how busy work is I could maybe go up for a few days. Like Monday–Thursday or something like that.

Me

Orrrrrr I buy you a ticket and you road trip with me on Monday from Reno to the bridge, we jump a shit load . . . and then I drop you at the airport in Utah whenever you have to go.

John

Damn. You're either just super spontaneous and awesome . . . or crazy as fuck n I need to be careful

Me

Probably a bit of both

I just live a really fast life, and if I can logically justify stuff then it makes sense to me

For example, this is my first time going back to the bridge and I'm hella fucking nervous . . . Matt can't come with me because he has to be in San Francisco with his brother, Sean I think is already in Europe, and so I want somebody who I know is a good BASE jumper and who I trust to stand next to me at that exit for at least the next few jumps . . . so the way I see it buying you a ticket is actually a cheaper way of getting a BASE instructor/buddy to join me.

Me

Seeeeee it's logic!

Me

I'm probably not making a very good argument for the anti-crazy, but my life is just pretty wild, so if I want to get to know somebody more they kinda have to jump along for the ride once in while

John

I can see the logic in your crazy
I can relate to that a lot as well cause I'm always on the move n it's hard to find people on the same pace.

John

My only hangup is not having my house with me

Me

Wait, you've never moved in with a girl after meeting her for five minutes?

Me

I just think it's like kind of a massive waste of driving to go all the way from SoCal to the bridge and back for 2/3 days when you can just fly n ride with me.

John

Ok, fuck it, let's do it.

Me

Awesome!

John

☺
But no I've never moved in with someone that quick haha

Me

All right so my suggestion would be that you just leave your car at Perris and drive back to LA with me Sunday night, crash at my place, we fly out Monday morning to Reno, pick up my van, and head to the bridge. Then you can fly back into San Diego, or Orange County, or whatever's closest and have a buddy pick you up.

So really it's only like I don't know . . . a few days of living together, just enough time to really get sick of each other and want to push each other off a bridge

John

You're awesome.

Me

Dope! I'll see you Sunday. Send me your full name and date of birth

John

I could be a terrible BASEjumper though
John McEvoy
01-17-85

Me

No you're not, I did my research.

Me

**PLANE TICKET CONFIRMATION
SCREEN SHOT**

John

You don't fuck around do you

Me
Not really my style, life's too short.

John
This is already a great story haha

A Few Days Later...

John
If you don't have plans Saturday, let me take you out to dinner.

Me
Okay.

John
That'll give me a chance to decide if you are truly crazy or not haha

Me
I mean I think you already established I'm a little bit crazy, but everyone's a little bit crazy. I'm just crazy in a good way.

John
I like to think that I can rationalize my craziness and in turn I become the most logical person ever.

Me
Lol yeah sounds like me.

Me

Just out of curiosity, where would we go to dinner? there's like a total of five places in Perris and they're all kind of shitty food lol

John

First part of my idea was to ask you to go, haven't figured out where cause I rarely eat out.

I typically just make commitments and figure out details after.

Me

I'm definitely more of a "just do it and don't talk about it" kinda person in case you can't tell.

I have always been more of an action person — I guess that's part of the reason I'm pursuing BASE.

John

Ok sweet. I'm stoked to get deep on all this.

I'm really bad at texting and just with general communication so I've been trying to save the real talk about BASE for when we are in person. But can I ask what are you most scared of? Like when you think about jumping what fear related thing pops into your head first?

Me

I have a strong feeling I'm not going to come out of this sport alive.

And so I question why I continue to pursue it.

John

I totally get that feeling, and the questioning.

Did you have anything similar with skydiving?

Me

No but I used to when I started. So that's why I'm willing to explore BASE a little more.

John

Funny how you said you're a "just do it" kinda person cause I think you're a lot more calculated than you're giving yourself credit for.

Me

How so?

John

Aside from being death camped you've taken a course, are doing ballon jumps in prep for Europe, and instead of just showing up in Twin you got someone with experience to go with you.

John

But I could also argue that meeting some guy in a trailer park then kidnapping him is a risky move

Me

hey hey — you were vetted, thank you very much!

John

Haha, you were too fyi

Entering the restaurant in Temecula, California, my palms are sweating. It's strange because at twenty-eight, I have been on my fair share of dates and didn't seem to get nervous for any of the other ones. But this one is different; there is something unique about this man, I can feel it. The date goes surprisingly well, and by the end of the evening we are curled up in his van together, just laying on the bed looking at his ceiling and discussing our dreams and desires. Before I know it he is gently brushing the loose strand of hair from my face. As his fingers trace my face, he slowly leans in, his lips gracing mine. One gentle kiss before we fall asleep in each other's arms.

BLUE SKIES BLACK DEATH

John and I fly to Reno and pick up my van before driving up to the bridge. This is the first time back to the bridge since my BASE course, and quite honestly, I'm terrified. On the drive up, the fear of getting there is far worse than the actual jump itself, or series of jumps for that matter. I want to do a PCA on my first jump after a few months off, just to get the sensation back.

I'm trying desperately to keep my concentration on BASE and preparing for Europe, but there's something intoxicating about this man. Yet at the same time, unlike my previous stints of intoxication, this one seems to come with ease. Our moments together are raw. I can't help but think that this is going to be a wild ride that ends in heartbreak. But some of those are worth it. "Blue Skies, Black Death," as they say in the industry. Blue Skies — riding the highs that the human experience has to offer. Black Death — the lows that come to us all. Without experiencing the lowest depths of emotion, the black clouds that can cover us all, how can we really appreciate all that the blue skies have to offer? I guess that philosophy can be applied to all parts of life. Even relationships, even if they're short-lived. To be honest, I don't know if my heart can take another round of that, but I think for him, I'm willing to try.

POWER OF POSITIVE THOUGHTS

Standing on the wrong side of the railing of the bridge, my toes peek over the all too familiar depths of the river below. This PCA is just as terrifying as it was on the first jump course. I checked conditions like Sean Chuma taught me. I watched the wind patterns. I'm clear on all safety aspects — now it's just emotional fear, illogical fear. I take a deep breath and look into the eyes of the man quickly becoming my Irish lover. A sense of safety comes over me, as I give him a nod.

My eyes remain on the horizon, for I know that if I look down, my irrational fear will overcome me. *What if I die?* I think, and immediately squashed the thought in my mind. For I know that my thoughts are overtaking my body in this moment, and if they are negative, it may result in a negative jump . . . leading to my untimely demise.

What if I live and have the most incredible sensation and freefall? What if I trust myself? What if I trust my equipment and my gear and the surroundings in this beautiful landscape? Twin Falls is beautiful, and the Perrine Bridge overlooks the rushing river below, with the echoes of the noise cascading behind me as the trucks whiz past on the road. The two towering canyon walls are like columns on either side of this cathedral.

I take a deep breath and look down to confront my fear. *I got this*, I think to myself, and then look up again to the horizon.

It's late morning and the crisp air holds a hint of humidity. I take another deep breath in as the warmth fills my lungs. I let it out slowly, both hands clenching the rail. The backs of my feet pressed against the concrete and my toes dangling above the abyss. Three . . . Two . . . One. Focus. My breath is still. And I feel the parachute extracting from the back of my neck. I can feel it through the sides of my body. It opens above, and without a second of hesitation, I look up to grab my rear risers to correct my positioning, pull my toggles down, and steer into the landing zone.

A clean and smooth jump, followed by one of the smoothest landings I have ever had. And just like that, all the previous jumps and knowledge come rushing back to me.

JUMP. EAT. FUCK. REPEAT.

We've done seven jumps off the bridge so far. The inbetween of jump hours consist of yoga classes, river swims, and long sessions of making love in the van.

Sometimes I question if I'm falling in love with the experience or with the man. Perhaps it's a bit of both, and there's nothing quite wrong with that. Perhaps I should just let myself fall. Because what's the point of being engaged in this lifestyle if I'm not willing to sacrifice or to risk one of the great things of my life — my heart.

I want to stay alive. I think it's important to say that in this journey, I want to stay alive. There are many people who flimsy their way through it, and I question their intentions when it comes to something like BASE. But I don't question my own. I value my life. I love this life I have created. My time on this earth is precious to me, and I will do everything possible within my power to remain here. But when Dad and Denali were taken from this earth, I made myself a promise: I will not live my life based on fear. I will not shy away from fear, I will not let it control me or my actions. There's such a beauty in intimacy with fear. There's such a beauty in knowing that I'm afraid and being able to push through it anyway. Something so powerful in the recognition of fear in oneself. Was I living before or simply existing? I don't have to question that now. The highest highs and the lowest lows. I don't have to question that now.

By the end of the seven days with John, we have decided we don't want to be apart for the summer and he will join me in Italy. I'm fully aware that this story sounds irrational and wild, but so many signs led to this moment of deciding that this was the man I would spend the rest of my life with. On the plane to Italy, we talked through all the necessary questions I would have for someone I planned to commit my life to: How do you feel about marriage? Do you want children? Where do you want to live? How much debt do you have? How much money is in your account? Can we build a life together? How do you feel about me traveling all the time? Do you get jealous easily? What are your main insecurities? How will something like BASE jumping factor into our lives? By the time the plane touched down in Milan, there was no question in my mind. I knew clear as day, this was a commitment that I felt confident in making.

A WHOLE NEW ADVENTURE

In the late morning of an August day, on the banks of Lake Garda in Italy, John McEvoy kneeled down on the rocks of a small peninsula and proposed. I couldn't have written the scene better if I tried, so I won't even try, I'll just say it was pure magic. There were no houses anywhere around, just trees and a beautiful cobblestone path leading out to some rocks. He set up the camera to take a picture of us. Got down on one knee. It was by far the most beautiful feeling I have ever had. And saying yes was one of the scariest things I have ever done. For someone who prides herself on independence, the idea of life partnership is almost too challenging to comprehend. Giving my heart, my life, my soul to another human being is beautiful but simultaneously terrifying. More scary than any BASE jump could ever be.

At 4:30 the next morning, armed with an Italian BASE Association tag and a single bus ticket, I and the five other students in Sean Chuma's class are ready for our next great adventure. John and I discussed the fact that even though he is an instructor, it's important to separate my terminal

BASE experience from our personal relationship.Terminal Base is big wall jumping — any jump with a delay longer than five seconds. The technical definition involves a slider which is a piece of your canopy, but I don't want to bore you with small details. Generally most people who pursue terminal do so starting with two piece tracking (which I am doing now) then move into wingsuit BASE). Chuma is instructing this course, and John is one of the many other jumpers on the bus. Although I am now engaged to a jumper, I never want my jumping to be "because" of anyone else. That happens far too often in the world of BASE. There's eight people per bus on a first come/first serve basis, and the first bus fills up quickly.

As Sean makes his way over to the bus, it's like that Eminem song: I'm nervous, but on the surface I am calm and ready. It's interesting because I have the same little tingling sensation that I got before previous firsts — the first BASE jump in Ton Sai, my first time in the tunnel, the first speed riding round on the baby hill in France. My first time in a wingsuit, even my first ever solo skydive. Even my first jump at the bridge. During the hour-long bus ride up the hill, I'm trying to keep my concentration on BASE and not on my now fiance. *How can I love a man so much in such a short period of time?* I can't wait to spend the rest of our lives together. I already started planning, and in that planning we discussed BASE as an aspect — how it would fit into our lives.

It was a given discussion as there was a BASE fatality here in Brento yesterday. A young girl in her early twenties had severe line twists and impacted the very cliff we are about to jump off. She died in seconds, her husband watching from above. I'm terrified of this sport. And now the terrifying feeling doesn't just come from fear of losing my own life, but from watching my fiance potentially lose his. Maybe it's when you love someone else more than you love yourself, that suddenly your choices become less selfish and with that the pursuit of BASE seems more selfish than ever. *What's the point?* Perhaps the questioning is simply my fear materializing due to the girl's death in this exact location less than twenty-four hours ago. Even with that in the back of my mind, I've made a conscious choice to hop on a bus, ride up to the top of a 3,000-foot cliff, and jump off.

First light is starting to appear as we pull into the dirt parking lot at the top of the hill and hop out of the van. The smell of the thick forest in Italy is distinct, and my senses are heightened, as are my nerves. The hike reminds me of the trails of Nepal, scattered rocks mixed in with thick dirt and mud of the earth. A little slippery over the roots of trees, and midway through we come to a clearing. The view is astounding. A sheer 3,000-foot wall of granite and limestone mix cascades down to the valley below. What an insane creation of Mother Nature.

All geared up and ready for my first terminal jump, my stomach is in twists. We follow the long line of fellow jumpers on the fixed lines down a jagged cliff. There are two jumpers ahead of us already on the exit. They exchange fist bumps and with a nod of the head, the first one steps onto the edge. Three . . . Two . . . One . . . And he's off, his white suit blowing in the wind, arms forward before a three second margin of a push back, and he's tracking away from the wall. Suddenly his canopy opens above him, and I let out a small sigh of relief. No matter who it is at the exit, no matter who's about to jump, those few seconds always have me holding my breath.

It's those few seconds between the jump and the pitch that make all the difference. Those few seconds between life and death.

I watch as he soars out towards the landing area.

IT'S A GOOD DAY TO FLY

Brento is like a skydive. Most people say it's the El Capitan of this part of the world, and it's the attraction that brings jumpers to frequent this small town of Italy. Granite grays blended with yellows and golds to create a tower with a perfect perch for exit. And God couldn't have made a better landing strip for BASE jumpers. A red carpet right to the end.

From our group, Adam goes first. He's Australian. A little obnoxious, but quite entertaining. He takes a deep track, and with baited breath I watch until the crack of his canopy resonates off the granite walls.

"Who wants to go next?" Sean asks.

"Me," I say.

Sean gives my outstretched hand a gentle slap, followed by a fist bump.

I look over for a split second of eye contact with my sweet Irish love. Does all this still seem necessary? Because really, at the end of the day, all we care about is love. That's all that really matters in this world. Whether that love happens fast or slow, the primal instinct is to find your mate. I have found my partner for this life, so why am I jumping? Am I still searching for something? I step out onto the edge.

"Make sure you put your toes over the lip," Sean's voice rings out to me. The soles of my shoes are worn and I know they are slippery, but if I crunch my toes I should be fine. My scrunched toes trip the curvature of the end of the rock. And I look down below to the daunting valley calling my name. A vibration of fear rolls through me.

Standing on the cliff's edge, I glaze to the horizon where mist and mountains have blurred. The newborn morning sun descending the valley, I keep repeating something that Matt once told me: "You can enter danger and come out alive — through fear and back again."

Three . . .

Two . . .

One . . .

I launch, pushing off from the balls of my feet. In my head I can feel myself counting — one, two, three, four as the rush of the wind cocoons my body. I can feel the speed pick up. My arms sweep beside me. *Holding in, holding in. Fuck! What's my count, what's my count? I lost my count. Pitch. Pitch.*

With an instant jolt, I look up to see the canopy above me. My hands are on the rear risers. I'm facing left a little bit, so I pull on my right riser and turn myself straight. The canopy is intact; no line overs, no twists, nothing. I pull down on my toggles, release them and start to steer the canopy in full flight.

With a deep breath of relief, I unlatch the top of my helmet and pull my visor up. Looking out on the beautiful Italian dolomites, then down to the lush green valley. There's a house with a vineyard I want to buy. There's a small lake with deep blue water. I can see pretty much everything from up here. And with that, I realize I'm really fucking high, and the reason I'm so high is that I lost my count. I pitched way too early, which, actually, I wasn't supposed to do, because if you pitch too early on this particular jump, you're still quite close to the wall. See, although the wall is concave, it doesn't slope inward until further down, when the jumper is about seven to eight seconds into their freefall. So in order to stay safe, you want to keep the track at a minimum of seven seconds. You don't want to pitch too early because in addition to being too close to the cliff, you are also flying too high on the canopy and you have to burn some altitude like I am now. I spend the next few minutes zigzagging back and forth in order to lower myself to the landing area.

THE BFL

By the fourth day of jumping I'm really starting to get the hang of tracking, and the fun of flying has semi-sterilized my fear. We have formed a routine of two jumps in the wee hours of morning, followed by a coffee at the bistro across from the landing area, followed by a refreshing swim in the nearby river across from the campgrounds. Lunch is made with the finest ingredients Italy has to offer and often consists of burrata salad and pesto pasta. I love to cook, and I love to cook for John.

Above all else, perhaps my journey of human flight was a path to understand myself, my fear, my desires. By truly understanding who I am, that has allowed me to open my heart in a way I never did before. Perhaps my journey of human flight had led me to this love story, embedded in the pages of a BASE book. Since meeting him I have been frequently hit with waves of fear surrounding our love and its potential heartbreak. *What if he dies?* It's not an entirely irrational thought, given he is an active jumper who has dedicated his life to the pursuit of the most dangerous activity in the world. Perhaps this is simply fear based not on the rationale of BASE's danger but the irrationality of the role death plays in my life. Considering two of the three main men of my life (the third being my grandfather) were taken by an avalanche while partaking in an extreme sport, it would make sense that I have irrational fears of losing my fiance.

Although this activity provides some of the greatest highs in the human experience - like the yang to its ying - it is also surrounded by darkness and death. There is this thing called the BFL. It's an acronym that stands for the BASE Fatality List. This is a list that holds all the information of every jumper who has ever perished while jumping. Reading through the now 377 names, you're hit with a daunting feeling that you never want your name on that list. While at the same time, if you are going to die anyway, why not have your name solidified in BASE history? Is it really BASE history if the name that no longer belongs to you is assigned to a body that no longer exists? I am fully aware how morbid this sounds to a non jumper. Ultimately the BLF is meant as a catalog of information so that other jumpers don't make the same mistakes as the ones who wound up on this list.

Four days ago, the young girl who died here at Brento was put on the list, and just yesterday the BLF got a new notification for a jumper named Brandon Chase. A guy who went in at the bridge, right in front of his wife. He was teaching her how to BASE jump. This is the second husband and wife duo to meet tragedy in the period of four days. Brutal. Even simply watching John exit the cliff is terrifying.

Below the announcement of the death of Brandon Chase on the BFL is a series of comments; many of them simply read,"Blue Skies, Black Death." A part of me feels like that statement is used as an excuse in the BASE community when someone dies. Essentially it is meant to honor those who have fallen, to pay respects to them while simultaneously reminding the current jumpers to be vigilant and aware of the ramifications. Blue Skies — the highest of the highs. Black Death — the lowest of the lows.

But I have noticed there's this thing that happens when someone dies in BASE. There's an endless stream of excuses that the community makes for that person's demise. For example, Brandon Chance, who went in at the bridge in front of his beautiful wife. He was stowed, which means that his pilot chute was stowed inside his main container. He held a long delay before he pitched — four seconds. Just to give you an example, at the bridge, the longest I hold is two seconds. Keep in mind I'm a total pussy when it comes to BASE jumping. Now, someone like John or Matt or Chuma will hold three or four seconds because they know what the fuck they're doing. Brandon Chance was a very experienced jumper. Numerous wingsuits and BASE jumps all over the world. When you Google BASE jumping in Greece, the number one picture that comes up is of him jumping off a cliff on Shipwreck Island. But even with all that experience, upon Chance's death, a series of excuses were made.

After exiting, Brandon Chance took it deep on his jump, four seconds of delay, and when he went back to pitch, he realized he only had a partial pull. In other words, he had a weak pull. He didn't fully deploy the pilot chute, which didn't drag out the main parachute. So after about three fourths of a second, he reached back again and fully pitched. But by the time the pilot chute came out, he hit the water.

BASE jumpers will immediately analyze the reasons for this person "going in." Going in means to hit the ground during a base jump. Through this analysis, pretty much every single reason will be brought up. Be careful when doing aerials. Don't get a bridal rap. Double and triple check all of your equipment. Pack properly so you don't get a line over attention. Don't take super long delays. Don't take it super deep. Ultimately they're all just excuses on why this person slipped up and that resulted in their death. The scary part of that thought is we are all human — we all slip up and make mistakes. I'm going to slip up. John's going to slip up. And if that slip up happens during a BASE jump, our names could be right next to Brandon Chance on the BLF.

When the stakes are this high, every little aspect needs to be overanalyzed. For someone like me with a "just do it" mentality, this is a strange concept to abide by. The idea that everything you do in BASE could potentially cost you your life.

When I look at accident reports on the BLF, I cannot help but think, *Wow, that person was stupid.* The reality is we can all be stupid at any given moment. For example, this morning, before my jump, I asked myself, *If something goes wrong in this jump, what will the BFL report say? What will be the ramifications? What will people find in analyzing my every move? What will they say?* "She was tired. She packed late at night in the dark. Her pack job was rushed. She totally forgot to separate her C and D lines of the canopy. On the exit she was nervous. There were all these signs that she shouldn't have jumped, but she didn't listen to them and her instincts were off. And that's surprising for somebody who's a climber and outdoorsy. If your instincts are off, don't jump. Something's wrong. Don't jump."

Perhaps this is the way jumpers justify the risks — the god-like complex that it will never happen to them, they will never be the one to make that little mistake that costs them their lives.

"She's got under 50 jumps. She was there with her fiance. They just got engaged. You can tell by the engagement she was reckless. He was helping instruct her. He told her the gear was fine."

Without a doubt, if I die in Brento, John would get all

the blame. It doesn't matter that I was in Chuma's group. It doesn't matter that we decided he shouldn't instruct me. It doesn't matter that he never gave me his opinion until I asked for it. None of that would matter if I die, he would still get the blame.

Four hundred skydives, a reckless start with a death camp, only thirty-seven BASE jumps, only ten terminal BASE jumps in a tracking suit. All of these things would add up to my incident report and ultimately, my mother's pain. For then, she would have lost both children. My future husband's pain. For then, he would feel guilt for telling me that it was okay to jump. My in-laws, who are so excited about our marriage and our future together. The rest of my family, my grandfather, my aunt and uncle, all of these people whose lives would be totally and completely shattered by my one decision in this split moment. Once I step off that edge, there is no turning back. To jump something that I did not feel completely confident in the moment of my exit — my ability to handle the situation as it presents itself. If I am wavering on my decision to enter the unknown, like I am on this jump right now.

My mind is not right. My fear over the fact that I packed my parachute late and in the dark is causing my mind to spin. My fear in this moment may have some logic in the emotions slowly taking over. There are a plethora of reasons to ignore my fear — the effort it took to get to the exit, the fact that I will most likely not have a ride down the mountain. There is a slim chance that I made a mistake packing, and that thought was still in the back of my mind. The last thing I want is to have my name appear on the BLF. This is the moment to see if I am really able to decipher between instinct — true gut instinct — and illogical fear.

I make the decision to turn around. And with that, I pat myself on the back knowing now that I can walk away from this jump. That doesn't mean I quit BASE jumping. That doesn't mean I've stopped jumping even for the day. It just means that I know that if presented with a situation where my mind is not right, I can walk away. I can turn around and walk away and feel just fine — powerful almost. Knowing that I am in control of my own decisions when it comes to this, or any activity, is above all else, freedom. Thus, I make a promise to myself: if I'm not feeling it on the exit, I simply turn around and walk off the jump, because now I know it's just as important, if not more so, than taking the leap.

ATTACHMENT

It's our fifth day in Brento and the big wall tracking course is set to come to an end, but John and I decide to stay in Italy for another two weeks. After the recognition that I can walk away from a jump, a sense of ease came over me — the realization that I am in charge of my own jumping. I can choose to say no, but the next morning, with the same fears entering my mind, I was able to work through the emotions rationally, before calming my mind and stepping off the exit. This resulted in a sense of freedom, allowing me to have love for each jump over the next few weeks. And rather than give in to my illogical fear, I can walk off the exit or work through the fear — both are viable options. Neither is right or wrong. I am not attached to either outcome, and both can result in clarity.

The idea of non-attachment is something that has been present in my life ever since my first meditation retreat. The Buddhist philosophy is that attachment causes *dukkha, meaning* pain and suffering. Thus, attachment will result in pain.

One of the most memorable text conversations I've ever

had was with Matt about attachment before I was even a BASE jumper. I sent him a friendly text message one day: "Hey buddy, miss you."

And his reply? "I try not to miss. I try to live in the moment, and not spend my time longing or needing something that is not there"

That's the thing about Blanc — he can be so deep while simultaneously appearing ridiculous. That particular text encouraged me to send back the eye roll emoji.

"I'd prefer not to have an attachment," he replied.

"That must be a very lonely life," I said.

Then he said something that will stay with me for the rest of my life, not just in BASE, but carried with me every day always.

"You start BASE jumping, and you'll find out."

After Italy, John and I head to Chamonix to spend a little time climbing in the mountains before flying to England to meet family. Given we are getting married, I want to meet my future in-laws, and it just so happens my mother is also in England, which allows for us both to meet the family. England leads to Stockholm for the wingsuit wind tunnel (yes, that is exactly what it sounds like, a wind tunnel with horizontal air designed specifically for wingsuit training).

Then finally by September we are back in Italy.

By the end of my first BASE season in Europe, I finally

see why Matt Blanc said what he did about attachment. The summer was full of accidents, from broken bones to paralyzed bodies, and finally culminating in a BLF listing I did not expect. In a valley in Switzerland, Cullen slipped on the exit of a wingsuit BASE jump, causing his body to hit the ledge below. He died instantly.

Reading the BLF report on Cullen leaves me with a feeling of uncertainty in everything I'm doing. Jumping seems so pointless now, and I find myself distracted from the concentration that was so present before.

Facebook notes of "BSBD" (Blue Skies, Black Death) for Cullen seem like just a statement for those to justify the echo of emptiness scorned from loss.

My big wall jumps are training, but training for what? My ultimate death in this search for the blue sky in life? My body feels weak and drained, and I struggle with the fact that Cullen's death will affect some but not others. Others will still be jumping today. But the ones who really mattered in his life are left with soul shattering grief.

Other than Matt Blanc, Cullen was the first jumper I really got to know in this activity. It's hard to comprehend the pain his family must feel — a pain I know all too well. The questioning of a pursuit they will never understand.

And with that, slowly, piece by piece, I feel like I'm becoming less and less attached. Less and less attached to the idea of jumping. Less attachment to people. Perhaps the next step is to be less attached to life itself. Like Matt was saying, he'd been in the game a lot longer than I have. His exposure to constant deaths during the BFL season has been endless. I see it with some of my other wingsuit BASE jumping friends who have been in for many seasons too. The idea that non-attachment is the only way to live in a world where life can be cut short, in this game of Russian roulette that we call BASE jumping.

At some point I've got to ask myself, *What's the point of the human experience if I do not allow myself attachment?* With that questioning, there has to be a desire to understand potentially the true meaning of life. *Did the Buddhists have it right all along?* Life would be easier if I didn't care so much, but then what about love? Do I allow myself to be attached to my future husband, while simultaneously knowing it will only result in pain? My biggest fear used to be my death, but now within the matter of a month, for the first time in my life, my biggest fear is losing someone else — John. No matter what, he will die, and the chances are that the pain I will feel upon his death will be unbearable. Such a pure and clean love with the idea that I don't want it to end. But everything must end at some point.

As I ponder my life with John, the idea of non-attachment becomes fascinating to me. I begin to meditate on it. Meditation as separation from self and the sense of self. The idea of not being attached to things. Materialistic things, physical things, even emotional things. Don't be too attached to your dog, to other humans, to yourself, your body, to your eyes, to your feet, to your hands. Because if you can separate your sense of self from your attachment to this world and everything that's in it, you can flow, truly flow freely through the human experience.

When John and I talk about our future together, planning our lives together, discussing business opportunities, finances, land, houses, animals, children — these are all potential attachments. Potential pain caused from attachment. I start to think of the mindful selection that will go into this potential pain. Through this thought process, I come to the understanding that perhaps it's not wrong to be attached, but rather, it's important to understand and carefully choose what you are attached to. Just like with jumping itself, awareness is the key. Being aware and mindful of each action, decision and attachment. Thus, I mindfully choose John.

PART SIX

A LIFE TOGETHER

"I take great comfort in knowing that I'm nothing,
instead of thinking that I'm something."
— James Yaru

A WHITE PICKET FENCE

John and I were married in a courthouse in Houston, Texas, in front of my grandfather on December 27, 2019. Exactly six months to the day after we met. Following our summer in Europe, we went to my homeland of New Zealand to spend time in the country that holds my heart.

One of my most memorable BASE jumps I have ever done was in the South Island of Aotearoa. Just outside of Wanaka, the jump required hours of bushwhacking and even climbing through waterfalls before we finally spread our canopies over the beautiful green land.

John and I were planning a big wedding in John's homeland of Ireland, a castle and three hundred guests. However, during our visit with my grandfather for Christmas, he politely informed me that there was no way he was going to fly across the world. Given that I always wanted to have my grandfather at my wedding, we spontaneously decided to do the official ceremony that day at the courthouse in front of Grandpa.

It was beautiful, and given that just three months later COVID locked down the world and canceled all events including weddings, it was also serendipitous.

By mid March of 2020, John and I had bought a house in none other than Twin Falls, Idaho. I call it the farmhouse, and it's on an acre of land with numerous fruit trees, gardens, and even chickens. We are slowly creating our own white picket fence kind of life together. By the beginning of April we had adopted two puppies from the same litter and named them Ash and Hazel. Half beagle and half German shepherd their look as unique as their personalities. John was teaching BASE jumping at the bridge just five minutes from the house. I had acquired a distribution warehouse for my publishing firm, and by June, hired staff and was fully operational. Our life was turning into something of a fairytale. At least our kind of fairytale — a life we create ourselves, on our own schedule through our own terms. A life crafted for our ability to maintain freedom.

With the strange world that COVID brought, also came something neither John or I could have ever anticipated, something that turned our lives upside down, and forever changed our path.

On July 7th, John, at the age of thirty-five and in perfect health, had a stroke. The stroke led us to discover a large hole in his heart called a PFO. In addition to this, completely unrelated to the stroke and through the process of an MRI, we learned that John had a large tumor at the base of his skull.

I distinctly remember getting that call. The three words that no one ever wants to hear: "They found something." The same numbness that came over me upon receiving the news of my dad and brother's death stunned my body. Unable to move, I knew I had to be strong for John.

With decisive action, I formed a plan of attack and within weeks of John's diagnosis, we had a heart surgery scheduled in the city of Boise. The heart surgery was with one of the top cardiothoracic surgeons in the country. John and I had made the decision that we would tackle the heart first, as that was needed immediately.

The days leading up to and even through the heart surgery are still a blur, but the one thing that stands strong in both of our memories is the number 27.

John and I met on July 27th, the exact day of the six-year anniversary of my father and brother's death. Then on a spontaneous decision to get married, without even looking at the date, we tied the knot on December 27th. Now, the night before John's heart surgery, the Airbnb we booked was on 27th Street. We couldn't help but take it as a sign. A sign for what? We didn't know, but a sign nonetheless.

The night before the surgery I couldn't sleep. I stayed awake reading John's latest facebook post over and over again:

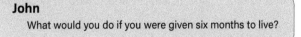

John
What would you do if you were given six months to live?

> **John**
>
> That's what I asked Sequoia when we were driving to SLC to get an MRI on July 14. At that point we didn't know I had a stroke, that it was caused by a hole in my heart, or that I had a tumor in my neck, we were still in the "wtf is wrong with me?" phase.
>
> I was kinda expecting her to start listing all the things she'd like to do before the end, but she just looked at me and said, "I would get a second opinion!"
>
> That's the kind of person she is. If someone tells her she can't do something, she just keeps looking until she finds someone who says she can. An admirable trait that has helped us a lot recently.
>
> Anyways, I have NOT been told I have six months to live BUT I have meditated on the thought of it a lot recently. If all options were exhausted and the hourglass started running, what would I do? I wouldn't run around trying to check off my bucket list or anything like that. Fortunately I've actually done a lot of the things I wanted to do already. I love my life, I love my work, and honestly, I wouldn't change anything.
>
> I would simply do more, of everything.

The eight hours of John's heart surgery felt like the elongated seconds of a BASE jump. All I could think about was the irony of my fear. From the moment I truly fell in love with this man, I struggled deeply with the idea that due to him being a BASE jumper, he could die any day. Never in my wildest dreams did I think that the possibility of his death would occur due to something as mundane as a stroke, a heart surgery, or a brain tumor. It sounds silly to say, but the idea of regular health issues killing someone who lives their life on the edge is almost unfathomable.

Due to COVID protocols, I wasn't allowed in the hospital at the time of the surgery. Thus my dear friend Lance and I played frisbee in a nearby park, a well needed distraction until I finally received the call that all went well and I could pick up my husband. Amazing that we live in a day and age where a heart surgery only takes eight hours and you can walk out of the hospital within the same day you are admitted.

John was strong, and that strength carried him through the heart surgery and the months of recovery that followed. Through the course of the medical memoir that was becoming our lives, we sought multiple opinions from multiple doctors regarding John's tumor. Ultimately, at the NIH headquarters in Washington, DC, after much speculation and testing, John was diagnosed with a paraganglioma. A paraganglioma is an abnormal growth of cells that forms from a specific type of nerve cell found throughout the body. It is rare. I mean really rare, like one in a million kind of rare.

Dr. Pachek, who leads the paraganglioma team at NIH, walks us through all of our options but given that it is not currently affecting John's life, we decide to simply monitor the tumor. For if it wasn't for the stroke, we would have never even known it was present in his body.

One thing I learned through this process of medical uncertainty is to always get multiple opinions. One opinion that we came to really value over the course of the next few years was that of a neurosurgeon named Dr. Lui. Because John's tumor was so rare, there were very few surgeons that we found who had operated on a paraganglioma, and although the tumor was not at the point now to need intervention, we both knew that one day it might be, so we wanted to be prepared.

Dr. Liu is an international leader in skull base surgery and complex tumors in the brain, skull base, and spinal cord. He came highly recommended, and our conversations with him reassured John that he was making the right decision to not have the tumor removed until absolutely necessary. My concern lies in the fact that the tumor could grow, and that would just make the surgery more complicated. John and I shared long talks about the possibilities and decided that he would get frequent MRIs mailed to Dr. Pachak and Dr. Liu for monitoring.

To be honest, the whole thing feels like a ticking time bomb just waiting to go off.

NOMADIC ITCH

The years that follow John's diagnosis and heart surgery are filled with love, laughter, and wonderful memories. Ash and Hazel are fully grown now, and feral just like us. Our beautiful family of four has provided stability and attachment in a way that I could have never imagined for my life.

"I" transformed to "we," while simultaneously allowing me to hold on to my independence. I couldn't have asked for a better partner in life. Staring at him now in the evening May light of our upstairs bedroom, four years after we met, I'm more in love with him than ever.

Over the last few months, we came to the decision that we are going to move to Italy, to the area of Brento where we first agreed to spend the rest of our lives together. Our nomadic feet are getting itchy in Idaho, and all of John's family remains in Europe. This is a chance for a new beginning, and given everything we have been through, we are both ready for a new chapter. The fear of losing John no longer runs rampant in my mind, nor does the fear of death during my weekly jumps at the local bridge.

Occasionally I will still feel the exciting tingle of fear through all aspects of life, whether exiting cliffs in Brazil or receiving the results from John's latest MRI. But ultimately I am now able to navigate that fear in a whole new way. A sense of understanding that I never had before, that sees me through even the most challenging of times.

That very evening, while lying in bed looking at houses in Italy, I received a call that my grandfather was not doing well.

ICE CREAM HEALS ALL

For three weeks I do not leave my grandpa's side. I read to him, feed him, help the hospice nurses bath him, and at night I sleep on the floor beside him. If you have never watched over someone on their deathbed, it's a fascinating experience. It's like I'm witnessing what it would be like to move on to heaven, and also simultaneously, what it would be like to move on to hell. It's very strange. Though at night Grandpa continues to reach up to the sky constantly. He has moments of clarity transferring in and out of what we consider reality.

Just as they are in the beginning, human emotions are very present in the end of someone's life. There are moments of pure fear — and for someone who has never taken the time to understand their emotions, it can be terrifying. I'd gladly argue that the greatest fear that most humans have, is the fear of the unknown. One thing I have significant experience with in my years on this earth is navigating the unknown, or what I have learned from BASE, preparing as much as you can, before then surrendering to the unknown.

With my grandfather, I sometimes feel like I'm guiding someone through death. Like I'm a teacher, even though I've never done it myself and don't know anything about it. If you are a person who doesn't believe that anything happens after life, I suggest you sit with someone while they're dying. In Western culture we tend to simply pump people with morphine to numb them until they are gone, but Grandpa was adamant when he told me he didn't want any drugs, thus I do my best to adhere to his request. Although not in pain, he will often cry out at night, mainly out of fear. Even through the process of a natural death, fear has a powerful control over us mere mortals.

I sit beside him and attempt to help him navigate the fear, I ask him what it is he is scared of? What he sees? Who he is talking to? I try to be patient when others tell me he's just hallucinating and needs medication. For I can see the fear in their eyes when they say the words "Just give him the drugs, it will all be over soon." It's in moments like this, I feel as a society we have drifted so far away from a connection to our own emotions. If we are not connected to our own emotions, what is the point of the human experience? It's easier to numb ourselves with drugs, and technology, than it is to connect with our emotions and nature.

The very strange thing no one tells you about people on their deathbed is that you never really know when they are actually going to die. For example, just today, Grandpa almost died three times. In the morning, mid-day, and now, tonight. All the signs of death are apparent, slow breathing, pale skin. I feel like he's been on the edge every single time yet something pulls him back, and within a few days, he appears again. This is an ongoing process that the movies and the books never seem to discuss in detail. In a strange way, it's very beautiful to watch the process the mind and body naturally go through, even weeks before death.

Grandpa sees things that are not apparent to the naked eye. I hear him softly moaning, and I ask him what he sees. "Colors. There are colors everywhere."

My grandpa Joe is not what I would define as a spiritual man, but rather has lived his life in a more practical way. He has lived an admirable life providing for his family. If I told him he was lying in a bed talking about the colors dripping down the walls like ice cream, he would tell me "it's hogwash." The other day he saw a man outside the window with long hair who just watched him, sometimes smiling, before simply going away. We're on the eleventh floor of a skyscraper with no balcony under the windows. At one point he told me about his kitty cat in the room. Curious about what he was experiencing, I asked him, "Where's the cat?"

He replied, "Right here next to me," as he patted the air beside him. He was talking about his cat that had died the year before.

Through the course of the three weeks I stayed beside him, it became like taking a trip with my grandfather, just he and I. On this trip, he could see everything, but was scared. And I could see nothing, but was calm. I distinctly remember the night Denali came to visit him. I was asleep on the floor beside his bed, and woke to the sound of a gentle whisper: "Denali." I slowly moved to the chair beside his bed. Again he whispered, "Denali." His eyes closed with soft breaths. He gently whispered again, "Denali, who are you with?"

Grandpa looked so peaceful and content in his own reality, until suddenly, he grabbed my hand tight and pulled both our hands in the air, almost to shield his face. "No, no, no," he cried out. "Don't let them take me. Help me, help me!" He kept grabbing my hand, his grip stronger than in previous days. "Pull me up. Pull me up!" It was almost like watching someone being dragged into hell. He was terrified. Shaking. Bracing himself on the side of the bed before reaching up again to shield his face. "Who do I have to pay to get out of here?" he shouts in his weak voice. "I'm not ready, I'm not ready." I can feel the fear emanating from him. I try to calm the energy and talk him through the journey, but those who do not try and understand their fear in life have a hard time with fear taking over in the process of death.

It takes time before grandpa is calm again. His agitation

subsiding, I play him some of his favorite music - Brahms concerto in d minor. My grandfather, an avid violinist himself, only ever listened to classical music. The melody smooths the strain on his face. When in the trance of the final weeks of death, it's hard to decipher when the body is actually sleeping. But his gentle breath and relaxed body, let me know it's okay for me to crawl back into my pile of blankets on the carpet floor.

In the wee hours of the next morning, I receive a call from John that the dreaded day has finally come. The latest MRI scan reveals that the tumor is growing at a dangerous rate and a surgery would need to be scheduled right away. I know what I must do. There is no question in my mind, and if my grandfather was lucid, he would understand and agree with my decision.

My suitcase packed by the door, I kneel beside his bed, to read to him before I depart.

"I wrote this for you when I first started BASE jumping, and now that I know you are leaving this earth before me, I'd like to read it to you."

Dear Grandpa,

If you are reading this it means I am no longer on this earth, and for that, I am truly sorry. I am writing you this letter not to attempt to explain my life to you, as this is a lifestyle that I know you will never understand. But rather,

I am writing this letter to say thank you. Thank you for believing in me when no one else did. Thank you for the years of turmoil I put you through. Thank you for understanding that my path had to be walked in a way different than most, and although you never could comprehend why I made the choices I did, you were always there to catch me when I fell.

You lived an honest life. A good life. A life of dignity, duty and prestige. I am so proud to call you my grandfather. Your world is beautiful, but you and I both know it's never been my kind of beauty. That is what scared you most about me — that I would never be satisfied with that style of life, the comfort that comes with security. No matter how you tried to give me roots, I would always chase the wind. Unlike Dad, you didn't struggle with trying to calm my flame, but rather allowed me to burn my own way. And for that, I thank you.

Although I may be gone now, please know that in my final moments, I thought of you.

Your loving granddaughter,

Sequoia

JULY 27, 2023

Of all the places in time and space, this was definitely not how I imagined this day would be spent. Today is the ten-year anniversary of my dad and brother's death, and I am sitting in a waiting room as my husband undergoes the first part of a multifaceted highly complex tumor surgery.

St. Barnabas Hospital is located in Livingston, New Jersey, and is a beautiful facility as far as hospitals go. The surgery is being led by Dr. Liu, who is regarded as the best paraganglioma specialist in the world. A total of five doctors are needed for the operation that spans two days. All their schedules had to align, and when Dr. Liu informed us it could be any day over the next few months, we didn't even consider the chances that it would fall on this fateful date. When we received the email that John would begin the procedure on July 27th, we were both in shock.

On July 27, 2013, ten years ago today, my father and brother were swept away in an avalanche on K2.

On July 27, 2019, four years ago today, I met John. The fact that we met on the exact anniversary of their deaths was one of the many signs that this was the man with whom I was meant to spend the rest of my life.

And now, on July 27, 2023, here I am in an empty waiting room . . .

John is the most incredible human being I have ever known and holds many attributes of my father and my brother. The dedication of his entire life to the pursuit of his passion and career in an extreme sport that challenges him physically and mentally reminds me of my father, Marty.

His kind nature, overwhelming patience, and heart, remind me of my brother, Denali.

And most of all, John's presence in my life as my partner gives me the sense of stability that my grandfather always provided. His death just a few days after I left his side is something I still haven't had the chance to process, for my focus has been on everything leading up to this moment in this waiting room. *If there is a great designer of the universe, could he possibly be so cruel as to take my husband from me on the very day he took my father and brother? Or perhaps, the fact that the surgery fell on this day is a sign that everything will be okay, just like 27th Street was a sign during the heart surgery.*

After a fifteen-hour surgery spanning over two days, John is wheeled into the room where I have been anxiously waiting. A feeling of relief flows over me when he finally wakes. Dr. Liu comes in to give us a full synopsis of the surgery including photographs of the removal of the tumor, which was the size of a small lemon, from the base of his skull. Dr. Liu then proceeds to explain John's current condition.

"His voice is not functioning. He cannot swallow yet, that may return with time. But for now he will be on a suction tube for his saliva, so he doesn't choke." He pauses as he sees the look on my face.

"Starting in the morning John will go on a temporary feeding tube through his nose. The important thing is you just take it day by day and you will find a way through this."

THINGS TO KNOW

By day twenty-six, John has lost almost thirty pounds. Meanwhile, I'm getting fat on hospital food. This is definitely a roller coaster ride, physically and emotionally. Never in my life have I experienced the emotional turmoil of living in a hospital — I mean fully living in a hospital. Given we are placed in the tumor ward and many on our floor are actively dying of cancers and other things people are "Code Blue-ing" on a regular basis. That means they flatline with no heartbeat. The BFL season in BASE is no match for this hospital floor.

In order to maintain sanity, I have constructed a morning routine that consists of a workout, some fresh air and a coffee.

A few things I've learned since the start of our time here:
- After about fifteen days, hospital security just stops asking you for a visitor's pass.
- Every patient needs an advocate with them in the hospital all the time. Without that wife/family/somebody advocating for them, stuff gets missed.

- Essential oils are awesome! I've been using them under John's nose when he goes to sleep, putting them in lotion, even using a diffuser with them to make the room smell nice.

- "Is there anything I can do for you?" is incredibly overused, and very few people actually mean it.

- Most people who are dealing with a situation like this don't have time to answer what you can do for them. Our brains are scrambled; we're just trying to figure out how to make it to the next day.

- Tiger Balm is king.

- A daily dose of sunshine is important when living in a hospital.

- Eucalyptus makes a great gift. They're beautiful when they're fresh and still smell amazing when they dry.

- There's nothing like going through a situation like this to make you realize who you really want to keep in your life.

- Everyone has sympathy for what you are going through until they want something from you, and then they expect you to still be functioning as a normal human.

- Showing up makes a world of difference. We have had people jump on a plane from halfway across the country or halfway across the world. People drive nine hours just to take me to lunch outside the hospital. It doesn't have to just be your physical presence; any gesture of showing up — delivering balloons, sending flowers — is an amazing display of love and support.

• Don't take it personally if your calls are not answered or texts aren't replied to.

THE HEALING POWER OF LOVE

For the last month, John's physical body has been so weak I was scared to even hug him because I felt like I would damage him more. His body has been through hell. Even taking a few steps was a big effort, and when I would wash his body, I could feel every bone. Through it all, patience and love are the only things I remind myself of when I feel like giving up. Perhaps taking care of Grandpa prepared me for this emotional journey, and gave me the strength to pull through.

Between my grandfather and John, I have spent the last year of my life caregiving. For anyone who has been a full time caregiver, you understand the toll that takes on your mental and physical health. Not only are you watching your loved one go through something incredibly traumatic, you yourself are experiencing the exhaustion and fatigue of having to bear the intense emotions that come with the rollercoaster of human health, or in my grandfather's case, death.

My appreciation level for healthcare workers and specifically hospice workers has grown immensely over the course of the last year. But ultimately, I think it's important to be aware that for them, it's a job. For the loved one who sits beside a bed, it's their life.

John's the strongest man I know, and to see what this ordeal has done to him has been so painful to watch, but he's kept his mental fortitude through it all and continued inspiring me even in the darkest times. He simply surrendered to the healing process, and now his physical body is slowly returning. He's off the feeding tube and can eat on his own, and he's gained five pounds. I can finally see light at the end of this horrible tunnel. The little morning routine, along with what's becoming my life, allow me to feel a sense of normality in an otherwise dramatically abnormal situation.

Once a week I go to the local market to get healthy food and snacks for John. Our originally sterile white room on the second floor of the West Wing of St. Barnabas Hospital is now full of colorful energy. I made sure to have a diffuser with essential oils ordered to the room, a colored throw blanket, and even artwork. The eucalyptus sent by John's Irish buddies dried beautifully and adds a nice accent to the smell of the diffuser.

The purple and white orchids from our friends Scooty and Julia, along with the stack of balloons from JP and Andrea, make the whole room a place for healing filled with love and positive energy.

ART SPEAKS

By day thirty-five we have been moved to the fourth floor of the West Wing, and John has been cleared to take evening strolls with a cane through the long narrow corridors. Through the previous few months of the whirlwind that has been our lives, we came to a decision to put Italy on hold. Thinking that maybe the next few years should stay stable, remaining content with the life we created in a small town in Idaho. Perhaps this medical situation was the universe's way of saying our wild days of wandering are behind us both.

But upon moving to the fourth floor, during our evening stroll through the thin corridor, we notice the artwork lining the walls. Each floor of the hospital holds a different theme of art. On the second floor were beaches and waves, large printed photographs of the deep blues of the ocean. Here on the fourth floor, lining the walls are framed photographs of the lakes of Italy, and at the end of the corridor a large print of the narrow road looking out on Lake Garda. We look at each other and smile.

"Do you think the hospital walls in Italy have pictures of Livingston, New Jersey?" John asks.

"If that's not a sign, I don't know what is," I reply, as we both let out a little laugh.

FINAL CHAPTER

As I write this final chapter, it's been almost eight months since John's tumor surgery. It took many months of recovery but by January of 2024, John was cleared to jump again. My own relationship with BASE still exists but in a very different capacity.

I still feel fear; that hasn't changed. Now, I have just come to understand and recognize my fear — rational versus irrational — and I hold an intimate relationship with fear that allows me to apply it to other points in my life. Through this experience I have come to know and trust myself better than I could have ever imagined.

We spend most of our time traveling these days. And currently, we are in the final negotiations to purchase a property right next to Brento. Who knows exactly what the future will bring, but whatever it may be, I have no doubt about the person who will be at my side.

More than eight years have passed since I first started this journey of experiencing human flight and ultimately understanding my fear. Along the way, my relationship with jumping has changed dramatically. With the ebbs and flows of life, the dream of flight has brought and continues to bring unique experiences that cannot be replicated. But the greatest thing that BASE has brought me, without a doubt, is John.

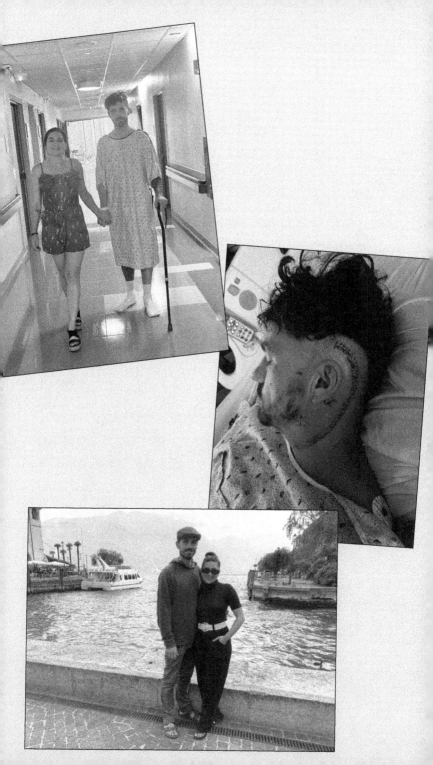

AFTERWORD

A Man's Perspective
by John McEvoy

Of all the things I've learned so far in life, it's that when your wife asks you to do something, you do it. So here I sit, writing the afterword to her third book.

I'm sure most people would say that when they met their significant other it was life-changing, but for me, it really was.

We met, of all places, in a trailer park!

At the time I was working for a couple friends who owned the repair shop (known as the rigging loft) at Skydive Perris. I was living out of my van at the time and would park outside my friend's trailer at night. So, technically, I was squatting in a trailer park.

It's kind of funny when told like that, but to be fair, it's not like we were down on our luck. My friends were running a successful business, and they lived in the park because rent was cheap and it was less than a mile from work.

One night after work, one of my friends brought Sequoia by to hang out.

I was tired and dirty after a long day packing parachutes.

We were all just kind of chit-chatting, and at some point,

things switched to Sequoia just asking me question after question about my life, my background, my future plans, etc.

At that point in time, I was at the tailend of a perpetual cycle of working for a few months while saving as much as possible, then I'd go on a trip, spend it all, and repeat. I did have a plan of moving to Moab, buying a storage unit, and running my gear store out of it. So at that time, while I didn't have any long-term goals necessarily, my next step was to do that.

I didn't go to college. I pretty much started working right out of school, and by twenty-five I was running a very successful fitness business and making six figures.

When I hit thirty I felt like I had missed out on a lot. I had just started jumping, and decided to catch up on all the things I wish I had done in my twenties.

So I sold my business, committed my life to jumping, and essentially became a bum by choice. While I've done a lot of things in my life that seem out of the ordinary, I feel like they have all been pretty calculated decisions. I didn't just wake up and decide to sell everything. It took me a year and a half to set everything up before I walked away from it all.

Fast forward a few years and I'm sitting in a trailer park meeting the woman who would become my wife a few months later.

We had a nice chat, but I didn't feel like we were flirting or anything like that.

Sequoia was getting up early the following morning to do a balloon jump so she left around 9:00 p.m. When she was leaving she went around the circle and hugged everyone goodbye, and after receiving mine, she said, "And you get a kiss," then kissed me on the cheek.

I remember thinking to myself, *Nice chick. I'll probably never see her again.*

I honestly didn't think too much about it.

A day or so later I received a friend request from her on Facebook and a message inviting me to join her at the bridge. I was kind of conflicted with the decision. I wasn't sure if she actually liked me and wanted to hang out, or if she just wanted to get free coaching.

After thinking on it a bit, I decided to just roll the dice and committed to spending a week in a van with this girl who I had just met.

I figured that if things went well it would be awesome, and if they didn't, I would have a good story to tell.

Then I started digging a little. I looked her up on Instagram, and when I saw how many followers she had, I thought, *Who is this chick?*

I saw she had written a couple of books, so I ordered both of them and read them before our first date. It seems kind of funny that I'm now writing the afterword for her third.

The night before we were set to spend a week together, I took her out to dinner and then to a movie, which was terrible. We actually walked out less than forty minutes in. I don't even remember what it was, just that we both agreed that it was unwatchable.

The following morning we did a balloon skydive together, which was an awesome experience, and everything just rolled from there.

We drove to Idaho from California together and essentially didn't leave each other's sight for the next week. Eating, sleeping, jumping, hiking, repeat.

Looking back, it seems pretty crazy for a first date to essentially last ten days straight, but honestly I highly recommend it!

There was no hiding. Oftentimes I feel like when you're first getting to know someone, you wear a mask and present your best self before some of your less attractive habits start to come out, but when you're with someone constantly you can't do that.

In general, when you're jumping with someone you tend to get to pretty deep conversations quickly. There's something about doing dangerous activities that brings what's important to the surface, and that was definitely true in our case.

At the end of the week she told me she didn't want

things to end and invited me to come to Europe with her the following week.

Another decision I was conflicted about, which resulted in me calling my friend and ultimately quitting my job. Again I had the thought of, *If things go well, this will be awesome, and if they don't I'll have a good story to tell.*

I flew to Europe and met her a short while later. I proposed at a secluded spot on the side of Lake Garda, she said yes, and the rest, as they say, is history.

Anyone who knows Sequoia knows that she does everything with 100 percent effort, and quickly. If she decides she wants something, she gets it.

For whatever reason, she wanted me, and who was I to complain?

Eight months later we were married and bought a house in Twin Falls with the intention of running it as a seasonal hostel for BASE jumpers. A week after closing on the house the first COVID lockdown came into effect and what was to be our joint business venture quickly turned into our shelter in place bunker.

Things in Idaho started to return to somewhat normal after a few months (not like more urban areas) and things were good, then — BOOM — I collapsed while teaching a course. I don't feel like it's necessary to go into a lot of detail here. Long story short, I had a stroke.

It was determined that I had a hole in my heart, which

was ultimately the cause. It was speculated that I got a blood clot in my leg, it went up into my heart and through the tiny hole, and then into my brain.

Completely unrelated, a tumor was also discovered at the base of my skull. A very rare kind of tumor known as a paraganglioma. I was told that only one in a million people get them. I always knew I was special.

I first recovered from the stroke with no residual after effects. Then I had surgery to plug the hole in my heart and recovered from that.

I consulted with a few specialist surgeons about my tumor and got some differing opinions. One said to get radiation, another said surgery immediately, another said to do nothing for the time being and just monitor things with scans every six months.

Seeing as it wasn't causing any issues, I decided to wait. The more cautious surgeon told me that I was in a rare bracket, already having recovered from the stroke so well, and I would likely have some problems if I chose to remove the tumor, so he recommended I enjoy my good health as long as I could.

Throughout this entire process Sequoia was the glue that held everything together. I'm the kind of person who will do everything possible to walk something off before I seek medical attention. Following the stroke I likely wouldn't have even gone to the hospital if she didn't insist.

She made all the appointments, did endless research, and dove head first into figuring out everything about this rare condition I was dealing with.

Needless to say, this was a lot to deal with for a couple who had known each other less than a year, plus it all happening in the middle of COVID.

Seeing how committed she was to doing everything she possibly could to help me during that time left me with no doubt that she was my life partner. I feel like the entire world could burn down around me and she would still be standing in the ashes with me.

The next three years pretty much went somewhat normal. I really don't know what normal means given that both of us live lives that would seem extremely abnormal to the majority of people. I guess I mean that we didn't have any huge problems to deal with.

In June of 2023, the results of my bi-annual MRI came in saying that the tumor had grown significantly and that surgery was now the best option.

A few months of planning and preparation led to having the surgery, and I ended up spending thirty-seven days in the hospital. During that time I was discharged twice — both times I was rushed back in less than twelve hours later. Once with pneumonia, the other as a result of collapsing and having a seizure.

As horrible as the experience was, I feel like it was kind

of easy for me because I essentially just had to surrender to the process and accept things as they came. I couldn't do anything to influence any outcomes, so I just laid there and followed instructions (mostly).

Through it all, Sequoia slept on the couch at my side and didn't complain once. I feel like it was a much more difficult time for her, but in true Sequoia fashion, she handled it like a champ. It was a nightmare to say the least. I will likely tell the story in full at some point, but I don't feel like it's appropriate to put such a horror story at the end of Sequoia's book.

Our story, thus far, has been one of love, triumph, tragedy, pleasure, and pain.

And I wouldn't want it any other way!

Once you have tasted flight, you will forever walk the earth with your eyes turned skyward. For there you have been, and there you will always long to return.
–Leonardo DaVinci

ABOUT THE PUBLISHER

Di Angelo Publications was founded in 2008 by Sequoia Schmidt—at the age of seventeen. The modernized publishing firm's creative headquarters is in Los Angeles, California, with its distribution center located in Twin Falls, Idaho. In 2020, Di Angelo Publications made a conscious decision to move all printing and production for domestic distribution of its books to the United States. The firm is comprised of eleven imprints, and the featured imprint, Catharsis, was inspired by Schmidt's love of extreme sports, travel, and adventure stories.

DAP BOOKS

DI ANGELO PUBLICATIONS